THE
DEVIL'S SLAVE
(El esclavo del demonio)

by
**Antonio Mira
de Amescua**

Translated by Michael D. McGaha
Introduction by José M. Ruano

Carleton Renaissance Plays in Translation 16

Carleton Renaissance Plays in Translation

General Editors: Donald Beecher, Massimo Ciavolella

Editorial Advisors:

Carleton Renaissance Plays in Translation offers the student, scholar, and general reader a selection of sixteenth-century masterpieces in modern English translation, most of them for the first time. The texts have been chosen for their intrinsic merits and for their importance in the history of the development of the theatre. Each volume contains a critical and interpretive introduction intended to increase the enjoyment and understanding of the text. Reading notes illuminate particular references, allusions, and topical details. The comedies chosen as the first texts have fast-moving plots filled with intrigues. The characters, though cast in the stock patterns of the genre, are witty and amusing portraits reflecting Renaissance social customs and pretensions. Not only are these plays among the most celebrated of their own epoch, but they directly influenced the development of the comic opera and theatre throughout Europe in subsequent centuries.

In print:

Odet de Turnèbe, *Satisfaction All Around (Les Contens)*
Translated with an Introduction and Notes by Donald Beecher

Annibal Caro, *The Scruffy Scoundrels (Gli Straccioni)*
Translated with an Introduction and Notes by Massimo Ciavolella
and Donald Beecher

Giovan Maria Cecchi, *The Owl (L'Assiuolo)*
Translated with an Introduction and Notes by Konrad Eisenbichler

Jean de La Taille, *The Rivals (Les Corrivaus)*
Translated with an Introduction and Notes by H.P. Clive

Alessandro Piccolomini, *Alessandro (L'Alessandro)*
Translated with an Introduction and Notes by Rita Belladonna

Gian Lorenzo Bernini, *The Impresario (Untitled)*
Translated with an Introduction and Notes by Donald Beecher and
Massimo Ciavolella

Jacques Grévin, *Taken by Surprise (Les Esbahis)*
Translated with an Introduction and Notes by Leanore Lieblein and
Russell McGillivray

Lope de Vega, *The Duchess of Amalfi's Steward (El mayordomo de la
duquesa de Amalfi)*
Translated with an Introduction and Notes by Cynthia Rodriguez-Badendyck

Comparative Critical Approaches to Rennaisance Comedy
Edited by Donald Beecher and Massimo Ciavolella

Pietro Aretino, *The Marescalco (Il Marescalco)*
Translated with an Introduction and Notes by Leonard G. Sbrocchi and
J. Douglas Campbell

Lope de Rueda, *The Interludes*
Translated with an Introduction and Notes by Randall W. Listerman

Girolamo Bargagli, *The Female Pilgrim (La Pellegrina)*
Translated with an Introduction and Notes by Bruno Ferraro

Leone de Sommi, *A Comedy of Betrothal (Tsahoth B'dihutha D'kiddushin)*
Translated with an Introduction and Notes by Alfred S. Golding in
consultation with Reuben Ahroni

*About the Harrowing of Hell: A Seventeenth-Century Ukrainian Play
in Its European Context*
Translated with an Introduction and Notes by Irena R. Makaryk

Antonio Mira de Amescua, *The Devil's Slave*
Translated with an Introduction and Notes by Michael D. McGaha
and J. M. Ruano de la Haza

Carleton Renaissance Plays in Translation

Antonio Mira de Amescua

The Devil's Slave

Translated by
Michael D. McGaha

Introduction by
J. M. Ruano de la Haza

Dovehouse Editions Canada
1989

Canadian Cataloguing in Publication Data

Mira de Amescua, Antonio, d. 1644
   The devil's slave
(Carleton Renaissance plays in translation ; 16)
Translation of: El esclavo del demonio.
Bibliography: p.
ISBN 0–919473–46–6

   I. Title.   II. Series.

PQ6413.M7E8313   1988   862'.3   C88–090346–5

Copyright © 1989, Dovehouse Editions Inc.

For orders write to:
   Dovehouse Editions Inc.
   32 Glen Avenue
   Ottawa, Canada
   K1S 2Z7

For information on the series write to:
   Carleton Renaissance Plays in Translation
   c/o Department of English
   Carleton University
   Ottawa, Canada, K1S 5B6

Typeset by the HUMANITIES PUBLICATION SERVICES, University of Toronto.

Manufactured in Canada. Printed by Imprimerie Gagné Ltée.

Acknowledgments

Both Professor Donald Beecher, co-General Editor of this series, and Professor M. Ian Cameron of Carleton University were involved for some time in this project. We wish to thank both of them for their help and invaluable suggestions.

The research for Professor Ruano de la Haza's Introduction was made possible thanks to a generous grant from the Social Sciences and Humanities Research Council of Canada.

This book has been published with the help of a grant from the Canadian Federation for the Humanities, using funds provided by the Social Sciences and Humanities Research Council of Canada.

Introduction

Biographical Note

Antonio Mira de Amescua, the illegitimate son of Melchor de Amescua y Mira and Beatriz de Torres Heredia, was born in Guadix in the province of Granada in Southern Spain probably in 1574. Between 1598 and 1600 he was awarded a doctorate in theology by the University of Granada. In 1600 he became *alcalde mayor* or mayor of Guadix. In 1606 he moved to Madrid, where he probably saw to the production of a few of his plays, among them perhaps *The Devil's Slave*, published for the first time in the *Tercera parte de las comedias de Lope de Vega y otros autores* (Barcelona: Sebastián de Cormellas, 1612). He remained in Madrid until 1610 when Philip III named him to the chaplaincy of the Royal Chapel of Granada. That same year, however, Mira entered the service of the Count of Lemos, Spanish Viceroy in Naples. He traveled with his new patron to Italy, where he resided until 1616. That year he returned to Madrid, probably in the entourage of the Count of Lemos. In 1619 he entered the service of Prince Ferdinand of Austria, who at the age of ten had become Cardinal of Toledo. A few years later (1622) he participated, together with Lope de Vega and Calderón, in the poetry competition held to celebrate the canonization of Saint Isidro, patron saint of Madrid. Mira remained active in the literary and cultural life of Madrid until 1632 when he took possession of the office of archdeacon in Guadix. He died in his native town in 1644 and was buried in its cathedral.

The Devil's Slave

Mira de Amescua's *The Devil's Slave* belongs to one of the most popular dramatic genres in Spanish literature during the seventeenth and eighteenth centuries, the *comedias de santos* or hagiographical plays.[1] They were popular mainly because the conventions of the genre allowed a fusion of the real and the marvelous which resulted in the creation of a fictional world where Good and Evil, reason and unreason, heaven and earth co-existed in a delicate balance. The *comedias de santos* guaranteed Spanish audiences not only strong emotions and a taste of the supernatural—very much like today's horror films, such as *The Exorcist*—but also a great deal of spectacular special effects. There is hardly a *comedia de santos* that does not resort to the use of stage and cloud machines, trapdoors, discoveries, and even fireworks. Raw passions, characters pushed to the limit of their endurance and involved in the perilous game of salvation and damnation, supernatural apparitions, special effects, and a dose of popular theology, constituted the basis of a typical *comedia de santos*, and help explain their lasting appeal.

A play like *The Devil's Slave* engaged a typical seventeenth-century audience on different levels and for different reasons. As the members of the Royal Council of Castile acknowledged in an "Opinión" issued in 1648, Spaniards flocked to the theaters

to see the decoration of the interior façade of the theaters, and the stage machines, as well as to appreciate the variety of the verse forms, the beautiful delivery of the words, the articulated speeches and gestures of the performers and the the entertaining comic scenes.[2]

In other words, they were attracted to the theater by the *mise en scène*, the dramatic situations, the poetic language, the acting, and the comic scenes. If we add to these five features the love intrigue and the fact that many of these plays appealed to a small but select part of the audience on an intellectual level, we will have the seven headings under which I propose to analyze *The Devil's Slave*.

1 *Mise en scène.*

By the turn of the seventeenth century, most Spanish cities of any size and importance had at least one permanent playhouse. Except in large metropolises like Madrid, Valencia and Seville, these playhouses were only used for short seasons, normally coinciding with the festivities of Corpus Christi or the day of the local patron saint. In large cities the theaters were, on the other hand, open throughout the year, except for the forty days of Lent, the Sundays of Advent, Christmas day, Easter Sunday and Whitsunday. Plays were performed in these theaters by professional companies of players, veritable commercial enterprises, sometimes founded with financial help from a capitalist partner. In small cities the stages were erected on days of performance in suitable enclosures, like the interior courtyard of a hospital or the main square. In other cities, such as Madrid and Valladolid, courtyards or *corrales* were closed off on the side of the street and fitted out as theaters. In the two Madrid playhouses, the Corral del Príncipe and the Corral de la

Cruz, some members of the audience stood on the patio, others sat on tiers of benches situated along the sides of the patio, the more wealthy watched from windows and balconies opened in the walls of adjacent houses, and the women crowded into the *cazuela* or "stewpan," situated directly opposite the stage. In Seville and Valencia, theaters were built *ex profeso*, with boxes on the sides and chairs fixed to the floor of the patio. The two most important Sevillian playhouses, the Coliseo and the Montería, had wooden roofs covering them in their entirety. As a general rule, however, the theaters were open to the skies with only a canvas awning stretched across, which served to diffuse the light of the sun (thus allowing the spectators to see the actors on the shaded stage) but that provided no protection against the rain. Performances were often suspended in Madrid because of rain.

Although it is quite likely that Mira de Amescua originally composed *The Devil's Slave* for performance in a playhouse in southern Spain, perhaps the one in Granada, the text that has come down to us probably reflects the staging conditions of the two Madrid *corrales*, where all important plays eventually ended up. According to the scaled ground plans of the Madrid playhouses, drawn by the architect Pedro Ribera in 1735, the central stage platform of the Príncipe measured approximately 28' x 16' and that of the Corral de la Cruz 26' x 16'.[3] On each side of these central platforms there was another smaller platform, which was normally used for seating spectators, but which, as J. J. Allen has shown, could also be used for setting up scenery.[4] However, as *The Devil's Slave* does not require the use of lateral scenery, it must have been performed with spectators positioned on three sides of the stage. Behind the central platform there was an area about 8 feet deep in the Príncipe and about 13 feet in the Cruz which served both as the women's dressing room and the discovery space. The men's tiring room was located beneath it, under the central stage platform. Above the women's dressing room, there rose two galleries or balconies, one above the other, and each provided with its own detachable railings. These galleries spanned the width of the central stage platform. A projecting roof, under which the pulleys and ropes needed to operate the stage machines were located, crowned this three-level structure, known in stage directions and contemporary theatrical documents as the *teatro* or the *fachada del teatro*.

Each of the three levels of the *fachada del teatro* had a set of curtains. In the section dedicated to the "*Comedia*" in *El día de fiesta por la tarde* (1654), Juan de Zabaleta makes explicit reference to the lower-level curtains (usually called *paño* or *paños* in seventeenth-century stage directions) when he writes that, having entered the female dressing room, his imaginary male spectator "looks through the curtains to check that the space to which he has claimed a dubious right is still empty."[5] Behind these curtains, a variety of stage sets could be shown to the audience. These sets could be extremely elaborate or very simple. They could be displayed on any one of the three levels of the *teatro*, but were normally set up in the central section of the lower level, which thus became known as the "*espacio de las apariencias*," or discovery space.

The sets used in seventeenth-century Spanish stages were not like modern "realistic" sets. Their function could best be described as "iconic," in the sense that they served to establish a conventional, analogical relationship with the places they were meant to represent. Thus, when in the opening scene of *Las quinas de Portugal*, Tirso de Molina requires that "the whole of the façade of the theater be from top to bottom covered with crags, rocks and thick bushes, as verisimilar and rugged as possible," he clearly indicates that this should be done "imitating a difficult mountain range."[6] The strategic placing of conventional objects, such as branches, imitation rocks, plants, tables, curtains, chairs, etc., behind the curtains at the back of the stage, established in time a system of codes by means of which the stage manager of a company could communicate simply and clearly the location of a scene to his audience.

The use of sets in seventeenth-century Spanish theaters is well attested not only by a multitude of stage directions, but also by contemporary theatrical documents. In 1609, for example, the actor-manager Nicolás de los Ríos, alluded to "the expenses incurred in decorating the stage and in stage machines, all of which are important to attract more people to the theaters."[7] In a document dated 1606 and bearing several signatures, among them Lope de Vega's, the manager Alonso Riquelme agreed to perform in the town of Oropesa, "*El hombre de bien, El secretario de sí mismo*, and *La obediencia laureada*, properly done with their decorations, interludes and dances."[8] In 1652 the police seized from the manager Jacinto Riquelme "all those things which they call decorations of the inner stage, curtains, ropes, peasant and buffoon dresses, pulleys, irons, and stage machines."[9] In this last document, the phrase "decorations of the inner stage" ("*ornato del vestuario*") refers to the adornment of the discovery space, which in seventeenth-century theatrical parlance was synonymous with the women's dressing room.

In his *El día de fiesta por la tarde*, Juan de Zabaleta alludes to one of the most common pieces of stage scenery in seventeenth-century playhouses: the mountain. Referring to the fact that actors spared no effort to please their audience, Zabaleta mentions that "if required, they would throw themselves down those fake mountains that they erect with as much despair as a potential suicide . . ."[10]

In 1675, the *guardarropas* (literally "wardrobe keepers," but used here in the sense of stage-hands) complained about being asked to pay taxes as if they were "altareros y tramoyeros" (that is, persons who adorned altar retables and *tramoyas*, which, I suspect, refers here to the platforms bearing sculpted religious scenes which are still carried through Spanish streets in religious processions, and not, as it does later in the passage, to stage machines) on the grounds that "our practice extends only to do the stage sets for plays performed in public theaters, in the Palace and in the Retiro, and also the stage machines required for these plays, and the carts for the Corpus Christi *autos*, and that if we have on occasions worked on an altar it was only because we were ordered to do so by the master craftsman."[11] This document is evidence of the similarity that must have existed on occasions between the appearance of a church altar and the internal façade of a theater, when suitably decorated.

By the end of the seventeenth century, the lessee of the Madrid theaters normally shared in the expenses incurred in the staging of an elaborate play, usually a hagiographical drama such as *The Devil's Slave*, for the obvious reason that they were much more expensive to put on. Thus, among the expenses incurred in running the Madrid *corrales* during the season 1695–96, the lessee includes "350 reals over and above the 200 reals which have been entered in the book, which is half the amount of what it cost to do the sets for *Santa Rosa*" and "200 reals, which is half of what it cost to do the sets for *San Juan Bautista*."[12]

As stated above, these stage sets (*adornos*) were usually erected behind the curtains covering the central space of the internal façade of the theater. This important space was utilized not only to display startling and spectacular discoveries and *tableaux vivants*; it was also supposed to function as an "inner stage." Although used more or less realistically on some occasions, such as when it depicted a cave or an alcove, the "inner stage" generally had a synecdochical function, in the sense that the part shown in it stood for the whole that the empty stage platform was meant to represent. Thus, a few branches and flower pots in the "inner stage" indicated to the audience that the stage platform, where the action of a certain scene was taking place, represented at that moment a garden; a bed in the "inner stage" meant that the scene took place in a bedroom, and so forth. The unknown English traveler who left a description of a performance in a theater in Cádiz in 1694 was in all likelihood referring to this effect when he wrote, "As for their Scenes and Ornaments, a Mountebanks Scaffold is an illustrious contrivance to 'em: Two or three dirty Blankets pin'd across the Stage, serves for the Curtain, that is the flat Scene before which they Act. And when they have anything to show behind that, they draw the Wollen Scene, and then the Audience may suppose what they will."[13] But, in fact, what the audience did suppose was determined precisely by those objects shown behind the curtain, which thus became signs denotative of the setting of a particular scene.

Another important feature of the staging of plays in seventeenth-century Spain concerns the set of curtains that covered each of the three levels of the internal façade of the theater. The existence of a discovery curtain on the lower level has been known for a long time. What is not yet generally realized is that the two galleries were also covered by curtains. The presence of curtains on those two levels may be inferred from a multitude of stage directions which require one or more spaces in the galleries to be used for discoveries and the display of stage sets. In practice, this use of the curtains means that in the seventeenth-century Spanish stage a change in the location of the action could be conveyed to the audience not only by the words of the characters but also, as we shall see in the case of *The Devil's Slave*, by the opening and closing of the back curtains.

A final feature of the staging of plays of relevance to Mira de Amescua's hagiographical drama concerns the use of a single stage set for each individual play. This set was placed in position behind the back curtains before the beginning of the performance, and remained there, with perhaps a few minor alterations, until the end. The set could be multiple, as in the case of Tirso de Molina's *La mujer que manda en casa* and Calderón's *La dama duende*, where different sections of it represented different locations, or simple, as in the case of Calderón's *La vida es sueño* and Mira's *The Devil's Slave*, where it always indicated the same location.[14]

Spanish plays of the Golden Age are always divided into three acts or *jornadas* (literally, a day's journey, because each act was normally expected to take place in the course of twenty four hours). This division into three acts was not introduced by Lope de Vega (Cervantes claims the credit), but it was established by him as one of the features of the *Comedia nueva*. Each act was in turn divided into *cuadros*. This subdivision into *cuadros* (the equivalent of Elizabethan scenes) was an unwritten rule, although the fact that dramatists adhered to it is made clear not only by the insertion in their manuscripts of horizontal lines at the end of a scene taking place in a certain location, but also by the way a play written by different playwrights was divided among them.[15] If this division has not yet been universally accepted it is simply because early printers of *Partes* and *sueltas* never bothered to introduce it. The importance of the division into scenes will, however, become apparent during this analysis of *The Devil's Slave*.

Mira's play is divided into acts and scenes as follows:

I.i	Marcelo's house in Coimbra.
I.ii	Street outside Marcelo's house.
I.iii	On a road.
I.iv	Marcelo's house in Coimbra.
II.i	Mountains.
II.ii	Marcelo's country house.
II.iii	Mountains.
III.i	Marcelo's country house.
III.ii	Mountains.
III.iii	Marcelo's country house: prison.
III.iv	Marcelo's country house.

If, because of their geographical proximity, scenes I.ii and I.iii and scenes III.iii and III.iv are considered single *cuadros*, then, as far as the location of the action is concerned, each act of *The Devil's Slave* is neatly divided into three scenes. More significantly, every second scene takes place in an open space, while the others are all located in one of Marcelo's houses. This alternation between open and closed spaces serves to emphasize the duality which, as we shall see, is inherent in the play's structure.

The text of scenes I.i, I.iii and I.iv makes no reference whatsoever to any sort of stage furniture or decoration. This is as clear an indication as we are likely to get of the fact that these scenes were meant to be performed against the neutral and multipurpose background of the stage curtains. The dialogue suggests that scene I.i takes place in an indeterminate room of Marcelo's town house, that scene I.iii is located

on a road outside Coimbra, and that for scene I.iv the action has moved
back to the interior of Marcelo's town house. The actual appearance
of these settings is, however, left entirely to the imagination of the
audience. Scene I.ii, on the other hand, requires the use of a balcony
with railings which have to be climbed with the help of a ladder. At
one point a stage direction specifies: "*Enter Lisarda on the balcony*";
shortly afterwards Don Diego tries to scale the balcony with the ladder
and, then, alludes to the balcony railings. In the course of this scene
characters also refer several times to a dark room, apparently situated
behind the balcony. But despite these allusions, no stage decor as such
was required for this scene. By simply drawing the curtain that covered
the middle section of the first gallery, the illusion of a balcony on the
façade of a house was easily created. The detachable railings of the
gallery served as the railings of the balcony and the dark room was
one of the lateral sections of the gallery, still covered by curtains.

Scenes II.i, II.iii and III.ii take place in an indeterminate location
in the mountains, but, unlike the scenes of Act I, they do require the
use of a stage set. Description of mountain scenery abounds in the text.
However, we should not conclude that everything described there, as,
for example, "the slope of the mountain" (II.i), "a forest of green and
dry oaks" (II.i) "the flowery banks of these clear little streams" (III.ii),
was actually represented on stage. As mentioned above, all that the
decoration had to do was to suggest the idea of a mountain range, with
the dialogue serving to complement and supplement it by describing
what could not be shown on stage. There are, however, at least three
elements in this rustic decor that are used functionally by the characters.
In II.i, Don Gil tells Lisarda to "hide among those boulders," and she
presumably remains hidden there until she confronts her father and
sister later on in this scene. Towards the end of this same scene, Don
Gil informs Lisarda that he is learning necromancy "in this cave." At
the beginning of this scene, Lisarda had actually described this cave
as "a cave of slate and different stones, lined with ivy and adorned
with vines." It is obviously not the sort of cave that one would find
in the real world; we are dealing here with a stage cave. In II.iii Don
Gil, referring to Don Diego and Domingo, orders his men to "tie them
to those oak-trees," and they remain tied to them until Lisarda "*unties
them*." Finally, towards the end of this scene, a stage direction indicates
that "*Lisarda takes out the coffer and jewelry from among the rocks*."

All these details give a good indication of how the lower level was
decorated: the central space represented a cave adorned with some ivy

plants and climbing vines with perhaps a few imitation rocks at either side of its entrance, while the posts supporting the upper galleries were dressed to represent the trees to which Don Diego and Domingo are tied. As J. E. Varey has shown, caves in the discovery space were a rather common occurrence in Golden Age drama.[16] In my article on "The Staging of Calderón's *La vida es sueño* and *La dama duende*," I mention a number of plays where rocks are used in a variety of ways and suggest that they were probably made of cardboard or pasteboard.[17] A tree with branches is required in Tirso de Molina's *El Aquiles*;[18] in Lope de Vega's *Porfiar hasta morir*, Tello hides behind a tree;[19] in Tirso's *El árbol del mejor fruto*, several characters sit under a laurel tree;[20] and in Guillén de Castro's *El prodigio de los montes*, Bárbara lies down under a tree.[21]

Scenes II.ii, III.i, III.iii and III.iv take place in Marcelo's country house, but apart from the discovery of Lisarda's body at the close of the play, they require no stage decor. In II.ii the use of deictics, "this countryside," "these fair vales," merely serves to indicate the location of these scenes. Scene III.iii is supposed to take place inside a prison-tower in Marcelo's house, but once again neither the stage directions nor the dialogue provide any evidence to suggest that there was any type of decor on stage. Thus, we must conclude that all these scenes were played against the closed curtains covering the back of the stage platform. The only exception concerns the "discovery" with which the play ends. In III.iv, just before the curtain is drawn, Don Gil announces that Lisarda's body "now lies among the myrtles in your garden," which seems to suggest that the decor used for the mountain scenes has undergone some sort of transformation: from mountain cave to orchard. In all probability, however, what the audience actually saw in the discovery space was the former cave metamorphosed, by the addition of some myrtle and perhaps the removal of the most obvious rustic objects, such as the rocks, into an orchard or garden, as indicated in the penultimate stage direction of the play: "*A curtain is drawn, revealing Lisarda's corpse kneeling in the garden next to a crucifix and a skull.*"

Thus, as in the case of *La vida es sueño*, *La dama duende*, and *La mujer que manda en casa*, and I suspect of many other Golden Age plays, only a single stage set, situated in position behind the curtains at the back of the stage platform, was required for the original *mise en scène* of *The Devil's Slave*.

Besides this stage set and the "discovery" at the end of the play,

The Devil's Slave also calls for the use of a trapdoor in III.ii, through which the skeleton which Don Gil embraces sinks out of sight; and at least one *bofetón* (or revolving stage machine) and two cloud machines: *"Angelio steps onto a revolving stage machine, which takes him out of sight, replacing him with the figure of a devil"*; *"An angel and the devil fight, suspended above the stage on machines"* (both in III.ii).

Trapdoors were used on Spanish stages from very early on. Cervantes requires one in Act II of *La Numancia*, and the early Sevillian theaters must have been equipped with them for the staging of Juan de la Cueva's plays.[22] Trapdoors could be opened on the central stage platform, the discovery space, and the galleries. Lope de Vega made fun of the zeal of stage carpenters in his Preface to the Sixteenth Part of his collected plays (*Décima sexta parte de las comedias de Lope de Vega Carpio* [Madrid: Viuda de Alonso Martín, 1621]). There a figure representing the stage appears complaining that he is full of holes, trapdoors and nails. The trapdoor utilized in Act III of *The Devil's Slave* was situated on or near the entrance to the discovery space. In III.ii, Don Gil, accompanied by Lisarda, enters the discovery space and disappears from view by walking off one of its sides. Shortly afterwards, he returns with her, but in reality *"embracing a skeleton covered with a shawl."* His avowed reason is that he wishes to see her beauty in the light of day. Standing at the entrance to the cave, next to the trapdoor, Don Gil then uncovers the face of Lisarda, sees the skeleton, drops it in horror and lets it fall through the open trapdoor.

The *bofetón* or revolving stage machine used in scene III.ii was, according to N. D. Shergold, "a device which either rotated or sprang to enable characters to appear and disappear as if by magic."[23] Its use was extremely common in all types of plays, but especially in hagiographical dramas. Its actual appearance and mechanism are, however, difficult to visualize or understand today.

The stage machines or *tramoyas* were platforms which, suitably decorated, hung by ropes and pulleys situated under the projecting roof above the internal façade of the theater. They were counterbalanced by weights that went through holes opened on each side of the two galleries, with the men operating them working from behind the back curtains. Most *tramoyas* were intended to move vertically carrying characters up to heaven and allowing angels to descend to the stage platform. But in some plays they were required to move horizontally or diagonally across the back of the stage and even to travel the length of the patio from the upper balcony to the women's *cazuela*, as happens in

Luis de Belmonte's *La renegada de Valladolid* where a ship carrying five characters sails to the middle of the courtyard.[24] Since in *The Devil's Slave* two characters are supposed to fight a battle in midair, their *tramoyas* must first descend vertically and then move horizontally by a combination of ropes until they encounter each other above the stage platform. The effect would probably look comic to a modern audience used to sophisticated special effects, but there is no doubting its appeal to a seventeenth-century audience.

Music is required on a couple of occasions in *The Devil's Slave*. Musicians on seventeenth-century stages normally remained hidden behind the back curtains, thus supplying literally background music.[25]

Critics in modern times are aware that the language of a play creates a fictional world with which it establishes a metaphorical relationship. But, in S. W. Dawson's opinion, "the nature of the stage [. . .], the settings, and the style of acting should [also] be such as to assist the language in its creation of this metaphorical world."[26] The preceding analysis of the staging of *The Devil's Slave* has, I hope, shown that this is precisely what the professional companies of actors in seventeenth-century Spain set out to achieve with the limited resources available to them in the commercial theaters.

2 *Acting*

Very little is known about how actors actually performed plays on the seventeenth-century Spanish stage.[27] On the one hand, the 1608 Ordinances regulating the performance of plays in Madrid imply that the period of rehearsal was very short:

Two days before a play, song or interlude is performed in public, it must be submitted to the Protector of the theaters so that he may see it and examine it, and it must not be handed over to the players for study before a licence is granted.[28]

On the other hand, there is the testimony of Juan de Zabaleta, who refers in his *El día de fiesta por la tarde* to "the thoroughness with which the players rehearse a play, which is a torment that lasts for many days."[29]

Two days seem hardly adequate to learn a 3,000-line play. However, these statements may not be as contradictory as they seem. Zabaleta is probably thinking of the rehearsals needed to learn a new play, but plays remained in a company's repertory for many years, receiving perhaps a dozen or two dozen performances during a typical theatrical season. Yet, every time a company brought new or old plays to Madrid, a new licence had to be obtained. Thus, the two-day rehearsal period mentioned in the Ordinances may allude to the time needed by the performers to re-learn a play which had been in the company's repertory for several years.

Be that as it may, actors could always rely on the prompter to refresh their memories. A prompter is always included in the annual lists of actors which managers had to submit to the Protector of the theaters before Easter Sunday. Since the Spanish stage was not supplied with proscenium, wings or prompt box, the prompter must have stood behind the curtains at the back of the stage platform.

Memorizing a play was also made easier by the fact that it was written in verse. Ad-libbing was probably reduced to a minimum, for, as the Madrid Town Councillors remarked in their 1598 submission to the new king Philip III, since plays are in verse, "the actor is prevented from saying what he wills and can only say what the poet wrote, and in this way the danger of having a dishonest and impudent actor say whatever he wishes is effectively averted."[30]

Lavish costumes worn by the actors on stage were part of the attraction of a theatrical performance, and also the cause of much envy on the part of the general public, who were forbidden from indulging in sartorial display by strict sumptuary laws. The 1615 Ordinances specify that "Players must not wear clothes forbidden by the sumptuary laws outside the theaters and the places they perform, but are allowed to wear them during the performance of plays."[31] *The Devil's Slave* requires the use of some spectacular costumes to be worn by the Devil, the angels, the Devil's slaves, Lisarda and Don Gil (first as bandits and then as slaves), the Prince, and others. No doubt this must have added greatly to the visual impact of the play in performance.

One of the best first-hand accounts of the actors' professional skills available today is in Juan de Zabaleta's *El día de fiesta por la tarde*:

Among the people who work in this country, actors are the most desirous to please the public with their craft [. . .] The first day of performance any one of them would gladly give up eating for one year to be successful on that one day. When they are on the boards, what efforts do they spare to play their parts as best as they can? If required, they throw themselves down those fake mountains that they erect with as much despair as a potential suicide [. . .] If the play has a scene of death, the performer who has to die, rolls on those boards covered with spittle and full of dirt, with badly fitted nails and bristling with splinters, as carelessly as if his costume were made of leather, and more often than not it is made of very expensive material. If the play requires that a certain actress should run off the stage, she flees with such swiftness that she leaves behind hanging from a nail a piece of her far-from-cheap vandyke collar, and her expensive dress ends up with a large tear. I once saw a very famous actress (she died not long ago) who, while playing a scene where she had to show rage, finding a handkerchief in her hand, tore it into a thousand little pieces in order to make the passion she was feigning appear the more perfect. Well, that handkerchief was probably worth twice as much as she made that day. Yet, because she was applauded for it, she tore a handkerchief every day while the play lasted on the boards.[32]

In Lope de Vega's *Lo fingido verdadero*, the protagonist, Genesius, a player manager, defines acting as

just imitation. However, just as a poet can't write convincingly and with feeling about love unless he is in love, since it's love that teaches him the verses he writes, it is the same way with actors. If an actor doesn't feel love's passion, he can't perform it. If he feels the pain of absence, jealousy, insult, the rigor of disdain and other tender feelings of love, he'll play them tenderly, but if he doesn't feel them, he won't know how to play them.[33]

Stage directions are not very precise about what is required of the performers, and contain very few indications concerning the way a scene should be played. Occasionally the dramatist includes comments like the following: In Tirso de Molina's *La joya de las montañas*, an actress is required to remain as if in ecstasy ("como arrobada");[34] in his *Cómo han de ser los amigos*, Armesinda pretends to be sad ("hace que se entristece");[35] in his *Quien habló, pagó*, the Infanta weeps and listens at times ("ha estado llorando la Infanta y escuchando a veces");[36] in his *Amar por señas*, Beatriz looks at Carlos with tears in her eyes, then turns towards Gabriel and laughs ("llora mirando a Carlos, vuelve luego la cabeza a Don Gabriel, ríese y vase");[37] in Ximénez de Enciso's *Los Medicis de Florencia*, while Cosme is reciting a ballad, Isabela must listen most patiently to him and at the end she must show great feeling ("a todo este romance ha de estar Isabela atentísima a Cosme, haciendo grande sentimiento al fin de él"); in the same play, Cosme makes many gestures of fear ("hace muchas acciones de miedo");[38] and in Guillén de Castro's *Cuánto se estima el honor*, Celia goes off stage somewhat weepy and upset ("sale Celia algo descompuesta y llorosa").[39]

As we can see, the acting style could well be described as passionate and emotional. A superficial reading of *The Devil's Slave* will show that Mira's play affords many situations for the display of the histrionic talents of the actors, to the delight, no doubt, of their seventeenth-century audiences.

3   Dramatic situations

Every successful play is made up of a series of dramatic situations. A dramatic situation must hold the attention of the audience, and awaken expectations of further things to come. *The Devil's Slave* has so many good dramatic situations that one can speak of an "embarrassment of riches." The following are some of the most memorable ones: 1) A daughter stands up to her authoritarian father, who wants to force her into a loveless match—a rather unusual occurrence in Golden Age drama where daughters prefer to feign obedience to their fathers while intriguing behind their backs. 2) A lover tries to climb into his mistress's rooms but is dissuaded from doing so by the impassioned speech of a saintly man. 3) This saintly man is himself tempted by lust and succumbs in a most theatrically effective instance of kledonomancy. 4) A woman turns bandit in the conventional way established by Lope de Vega in his early *bandolera* plays, but with the addition, as Melveena McKendrick has pointed out, of some original elements, subsequently imitated by Mira's successors, such as Calderón: "the lover's mistaken identity, the domineering father, the *disfraz varonil*, the robber boyfriend, the bandit gang and, ultimately, spiritual salvation."[40] This gives rise in turn to another series of dramatic situations, the most striking of which is perhaps that in which Lisarda, disguised as a bandit, attempts to murder her own father and sister. 5) A man sells his soul to the Devil in imitation of Doctor Faustus, but in exchange for a woman's love instead of for the gift of knowledge, and with the additional dramatic visualization of his transformation into the Devil's slave. 6) A formerly disobedient daughter repents and sells herself as a slave to her own father. 7) A woman and her lover meet in prison and each thinks that the other is a ghost. Any of these dramatic situations could have become the focal point of a successful drama. Packed together in the same play they carry an undeniable force in their cumulative effect, even if at the same time they make the play seem rather disorganized in its exuberance. Spectators in search of strong emotions and gripping situations would, however, find their fill in *The Devil's Slave*.

This accumulation of intensely dramatic and emotionally charged situations is partly what led Romantic writers to see the Spanish drama of the first half of the seventeenth century as a precursor of Romantic drama. For A. W. Schlegel, the vast majority of Spanish plays of the Golden Age were romantic pieces.[41] In Spain, too, Romantics such a Joaquín de Mora and Larra believed, according to Ricardo Navas Ruiz, that "Romanticism had been created in Spain during the sixteenth and seventeenth centuries, with their love for national literature, their opposition to classical rules, the mixture of tragedy and comedy, and the Christian spirit."[42] And in 1828 Agustín Durán in his *Discurso sobre el influjo que ha tenido la crítica moderna en la decadencia del teatro antiguo español*,[43] claimed rather hyperbolically that Spain's Golden Age had indeed been the true Romantic century. Even modern critics, such as E. Allison Peers, saw a connection between Baroque and Romantic drama.[44] I. L. McClelland, referring to their fondness for Golden Age *comedias de magia* and *comedias de santos*, commented that "the average eighteenth-century audience was as Romantic in sympathy as were the contemporaries of the idolized Lope."[45]

To be sure, there exist important and insurmountable differences between *The Devil's Slave* and the Duque de Rivas's *Don Alvaro o la fuerza del sino*, Gutiérrez's *El trovador* and Zorrilla's *Don Juan Tenorio*. However, there is no doubt that in its depiction of emotional matter in an imaginative form, in its use of images as vehicles of inner perception, in its attempt to express the inward and abstract by the outward and the concrete, in its awareness of the immanence of the ideal in the real, in its revolt against the strict observance of the three classical unities, in its mixture of the tragic and the comic, and in its fondness for the marvelous and the heroic, the Spanish drama of the first half of the seventeenth century may be profitably studied, and more easily appreciated by a modern reader, as a forerunner of the Spanish Romantic drama. Also, like many pieces of the Spanish Romantic theater, Mira's *The Devil's Slave* could easily have been adapted as a libretto for a nineteenth-century opera.

The Devil's Slave, however, is very different from the English Romantic dramas of a Lord Byron or a Shelley, which were in Lilian R. Furst's words, "dramatized poems that present a static series of situations without any real dramatic tension or conflict."[46] It does, on the other hand, share some features with the drama of Schiller and the Victor Hugo of *Hernani* and *Ruy Blas*, if only because of its predilection for antithesis and operatic effects and its acute sense of theater.

It is to be hoped that this comparison with Romantic drama, especially in its more accessible form as Italian opera, may help the modern reader to understand and appreciate how a play like Mira's *The Devil's*

Slave was enjoyed by an important segment of its seventeenth-century audience. It may also provide a way for rendering a modern production of this play more intelligible to a twentieth-century audience, better acquainted with Italian opera than with the Spanish drama of the Golden Age.

4 *Poetic language*

As T. S. Eliot once remarked, "without poetic drama we are cut off from the expression on the stage of some of the most intense and subtle kinds of feeling."[47] In the Spanish drama of the Golden Age, the expression of these feelings takes at times the form of set pieces—such as the three sonnets and the songs in Act II, wisely translated into English verse by Michael D. McGaha—intended to be enjoyed, like a good operatic aria or duet, on their own and not only as part of a larger whole. If we think of some of the speeches and dialogues of *The Devil's Slave* as arias or duets, we shall get a much better idea of how they were appreciated by a seventeenth-century audience. Don Gil's speech beginning "Admonitions, my friend, are bitter flattery" (I.ii), punctuated by the refrain "seek goodness and flee evil," is designed to arrest the action of the play and to be delivered as much to the audience as to the character to whom it is addressed.

In a prose translation, no matter how accurate and beautiful in itself, some of the poetic force of the original is inevitably lost. How can Constancio's brilliant imitation of a traditional Spanish ballad ("Señor si de tus vasallos" [lines 1708–35], translated in II.ii), capturing as it does the principal characteristics of this refined genre, be rendered into English? Regrettably, the poetic language which so enthused Spanish theatergoers of the seventeenth century must needs be debased in a prose translation. Yet, some of the force of the original can still seep through, especially through the imagery.

In the Spanish poetic drama of the Golden Age imagery ceases to have a simple ornamental function and becomes the operative carrier of meaning. *The Devil's Slave* contains several clusters of images, such as that of ascent and descent, worth studying in detail. One of the most interesting image-clusters is, to my mind, that concerning animals. Characters in *The Devil's Slave* are consistently compared to animals. The vast majority of these comparisons carry a negative connotation. Animals used for their negative qualities range from the dog to the rhinoceros. They normally denote savage and destructive urges and feelings: runaway horse (I.ii), furious bull (II.i), rabid dog (III.i), etc. At other times, these animals are seen as predators: carnivorous wolf (I.ii), "a hawk that scales a nest" (ibid.) "a snake, a harpy [who has] destroyed my nest" (I.iv). In one instance the eagle is used to symbolize pride (III.ii), and, on other occasions, animals in general (*bestias*) emphasize the characters' irrationality.

When animals are traditionally known for their good qualities, such as compassion, they are utilized in a positive way. God is compared to a lioness with her cubs (I.ii), and Marcelo sees himself as "a soft, loving stork" (I.iv). Don Diego, in his turn, accuses Marcelo of being unlike a pelican who would slash its breast open to feed its chicks (III.i). The proud elephant is alluded to because it "softens its fierce breast when an innocent lamb appears before it" (II.i); in the preceding act, however, Marcelo had likened his age to that same animal because of his strength (I.iv).

A third group of animals conjures up images of defenselessness and vulnerability, being normally used in conjunction with animals who prey on them. Don Gil compares Marcelo's daughters to chicks preyed upon by Don Diego, the hawk (I.ii); Leonor likens herself to a lamb who is going to be torn to pieces by Don Gil, the wolf; likewise, Constancio compares his daughter to "a little goat that bleats, craving the voice of its mother" when she is raped by Don Gil (II.ii).

Finally, some animals are used to produce a comic effect. Domingo, for example, considers himself similar to a "rented mule" (I.ii) because he can sleep standing up.

Animal symbolism is an effective way to convey an unequivocal message to the audience concerning the meaning and significance of a certain action. According to Marius Schneider, "while man is an equivocal, 'masked' or complex being, the animal is univocal, for its positive and negative qualities remain ever constant."[48] This does not, however, imply that being likened to a particular animal fixes the personality of a character or even the meaning of his actions. The comparison may be made about himself by a character who does not really know himself; or by a character whose feelings about the character being compared may affect the terms of the comparison. Marcelo, for example, is likened in a positive way to a stork by Don Gil and in a negative way to a pelican by Don Diego. Since both birds possess a positive connotation and for very similar reasons, the audience must try to resolve the contradiction inherent in these views of the same character. The use of animal imagery can thus add to the complexity of the play in a most effective way.

According to C. G. Jung, identifying oneself with animals "can be interpreted psychologically as an integration of the unconscious."[49] Most of the animals used in *The Devil's Slave* carry with them a series of archetypal and symbological associations. We may note, for example, that among the animals used for their negative qualities, the tiger is associated with Dionysius and is a symbol of wrath and cruelty;[50] the lion indicates for C. G. Jung latent affects and also stands for the danger of being swallowed by the unconscious;[51] the lioness symbolizes, according to A. H. Krappe, the *Magna Mater*;[52] the snake signifies hatred or envy in the Tibetan World Wheel;[53] the horse, according to Paul Diel, "est symbole de l'impétuosité des désirs";[54] and in the Egyptian system of hieroglyphs the owl was a symbol of death and darkness.[55] Among the animals used for their positive qualities, the stork has traditionally been a symbol of filial piety, the pelican a symbol of fatherly love, and, in the Middle Ages, the elephant was an emblem of wisdom, moderation, eternity and pity.[56]

The consistent use of animal imagery throughout *The Devil's Slave* emphasizes the animal qualities of some of the characters and contributes to the creation of that twilight world between reason and unreason, logic and instincts which, as we shall see, is such an essential component of this enigmatic play.

5   Comic scenes

Despite the fact that it is a dark and tempestuous play, dealing with important issues such as salvation and damnation, sin and redemption, *The Devil's Slave* has a certain dose of comic relief. Audiences expected it, and the dramatists always obliged. Most of the comic relief in Mira's play is in the hands of Domingo, the *gracioso* of the piece, a stock figure in the Spanish Drama of the Golden Age. His literary ancestors are to be found in characters like Onesimos in Menander's *The Arbitration*; in the slaves of some of Plautus's comedies, such as *Mostellaria* and *Rudens*, where Scerpanio, for example, is described as a "burly ruffian who treats his master as an equal" and Trachalio as "an ingenious rogue";[57] and also in the slaves who accompany the protagonists of Terence's comedies. In Spain the *gracioso* appears first as an important character in Bartolomé de Torres Naharro's *Himenea* and *Serafina* (first published in 1517) and in some plays of the Portuguese Gil Vicente (1465?–1536?).[58]

Domingo belongs to this category of stock characters, although, unlike some of the *graciosos* of Lope de Vega, Tirso de Molina, Ruiz de Alarcón, Calderón and particularly Moreto, his characterization is rather simple and his role in the play purely functional. As a character, Domingo is typically fearful and lazy, and shows a certain predilection for wine. His most important intervention occurs in Act I, during the "kledonomancy" scene, when he supplies the seemingly supernatural words that so affect Don Gil's conduct. In Act II, he tries to find out about Lisarda's fate and conveys the wrong information to Don Diego by telling him that she is dead, thereby contributing to the complication of the main plot. Later on he is captured by Don Gil, shows evidence of his cowardly nature, and provides some comic relief during the highly charged scene between Lisarda and Don Diego. In the third act, Domingo finds himself, together with Don Diego, a prisoner in Marcelo's country house, and once again his main function is to provide some comic relief. His reaction on seeing Lisarda, whom he and his master believe to be dead, is reminiscent of Catalinón's reaction to the ghost of Don Gonzalo in Tirso de Molina's *El burlador de Sevilla*.

Domingo, however, like many other *graciosos* in the Spanish drama of the Golden Age, fulfills another, and perhaps more important, function. By providing comic relief in some key scenes of the play, he succeeds, not only in presenting a comic perspective on events, but also in disengaging the audience from the fictional world presented on stage. In this way he opens up the intellectual and emotional gap that will enable the individual spectator to judge the characters and their actions. And this not because of any misguided attempt at didacticism, but rather because this type of play can only be really appreciated and understood on an intellectual and unemotional level. The *gracioso*, together with the artificial stage sets, the stylized acting of the performers, who never forgot that they were actors playing roles, and the fact that plays were written in verse and performed in broad daylight, contributed powerfully to the attainment of this effect.[59]

6 *Love intrigue*

For many critics this is the weakest part of the play. Despite the fact that Judith Rauchwarger and Roger Moore have, as we shall see below, convincingly demonstrated that on a thematic level the love intrigue forms an integral part of the overall organization of *The Devil's Slave*, the modern reader still finds the love triangle between Don Sancho,

Leonor and the Prince an unwelcome distraction. The truth is that Mira de Amescua included a love intrigue in his already overloaded play because his audience expected him to. Ever since Tárrega's *El prado de Valencia*, the type of highly conventional and stylized games that lovers play on stage held an enormous fascination for a certain sector of the Spanish seventeenth-century audience. They were probably attracted to the lyricism of some of the passages; to the expression of high-flown sentiments, mostly derived from courtly love poetry; to the verbal sparring between lovers; to the ingeniousness of some of the situations contrived by the dramatist, such as when Don Sancho attempts to speak to Leonor while the musicians sing; to the dramatic tension engendered by the rapid and conventional way in which the lovers fall in and out of love, feel jealous, flirt; and to the unlikely and sometimes daring confrontations to which this passion of love can lead, such as, for example, when Don Sancho disguised as a peasant fights a duel with his Prince.

If these situations seem contrived to a modern reader, he or she only has to think of the vast majority of pre-1960 Hollywood films from which, no matter what the subject, the love interest could never be absent. We are fortunate in that, as we shall see in the next section, in *The Devil's Slave* the love interest has at least some thematic and organic connection to the main plot.

7   The Devil's Slave: *An Interpretation.*

One of the first modern critics to comment on Mira de Amescua's *The Devil's Slave* was Alexander A. Parker. His conclusion was that "Mira's play is a remarkable work, but technically it marks a transition from multiplicity to unity of plot. The dual theme not only produces a crowded and rather disorderly action; there is no intrinsic connexion between the sensuality that leads Don Gil to sell his soul to the Devil and the disobedience and dishonour that leads Lisarda to banditry."[60] Issuing from one of the main exponents of the thematic-structural school of Hispanists, this indictment could not but influence subsequent commentators. For example, echoing A. A. Parker, J. H. Parker states in his *Breve historia del teatro español* that "the play lacks a desirable unity of action."[61] In his *Historia de la literatura española*, J. García López detects a "hasty succession of incidents and a plurality of plots within a single play."[62] J. L. Alborg, in a first reference to the play, notes that "Amescua [. . .] complicated the affair with so many intrigues that it is very difficult to summarize the plot," and later describes it as an "abstruse sequence of events."[63] On the other hand, Duncan Moir, in a more recent history of the Spanish drama of the Golden Age, has suggested that "incoherence of action, in an intelligent seventeenth-century dramatist's work (and Mira was certainly highly intelligent), may be deliberate, in order to provoke speculation on the playwright's motive in creating it; and incoherence in action may also be an invitation to seek underlying coherence of theme."[64] Following Moir's lead recent critical studies on *The Devil's Slave* have attempted to show that earlier comments about the looseness of its action and the irrelevancy of its subplot are largely unfounded. In 1976, for example, Judith Rauchwarger argued that "the secondary plot is found to both repeat and enhance the thematic development of the central story line." In her opinion, the "concern with yielding to a superior power—whether it be terrestrial or spiritual—is precisely what knits together the principal and secondary plots." This is why, as she points out, by the end of the play all the main characters have become "slaves" to a superior power, be it father, king, or God.[65]

In two articles published in 1979, Roger Moore also concerns himself with the thematic unity of Mira's play. He notes that the plot has a dual nature, based on the dichotomy between reality=good and appearance=evil. As he shows, this duality is maintained throughout the play at the levels of both plot and subplot: the play has two daughters, two sinners, and two interpretations, at least, for most situations.[66] As we have seen, this duality is also reflected in the play's *mise en scène*. The lush and artificial rustic decor used for the mountain scenes serves as the setting for the free play of passions and instincts, thereby adding a visual dimension to the equation appearance=evil; while the severity of the vertical posts and the curtains, devoid of any ornament, that form the backdrop for the scenes that take place in Marcelo's houses, where law and order rule, reflect the other side of the dichotomy: reality=good.

In a second article, Roger Moore concentrates on the role of Leonor, detecting a connection between her and her sister Lisarda in so far as "on the divine level, Leonor's subservience to the wishes of her earthly father is in opposition to Lisarda and D. Gil's disobeying of their divine father." Further, considering that the play may be seen as a contribution to the debate on the efficacious force of grace and good works, Moore concludes that "Mira de Amescua presents two central characters, one of whom is saved by divine grace (Don Gil) and the other by good works (Lisarda). These in turn contrast with Leonor, the obedient central character of the secondary action."[67]

There is no doubt that these studies serve not only to enhance our understanding of the play, but also to make *The Devil's Slave* appear much more carefully crafted than might have been supposed after a first reading. However, a play as vital, ebullient, and full of incident as Mira's creation seems somehow to rebel against being forced into the straightjacket of a commonplace moral or religious message. The straightjacket may be there, but it cannot contain the play; it is visibly bursting at the seams.

Let us examine the most encompassing of these moral lessons, the need to yield to a superior power. This is exemplified in the action of the play by the characters of Lisarda, Don Sancho and Don Gil. Each of these characters is seen to illustrate a different aspect of this central theme: obedience to one's father (Lisarda), to the king (Don Sancho), and to God (Don Gil). However, a close reading of the play will reveal that these aspects of the theme of obedience/disobedience actually raise more questions than they answer.

The ending of the play seems to imply that Lisarda's problems stem from the fact that she did not blindly obey her father. As Don Gil categorically states: "Lisarda was disobedient, but she has become so obedient that she is [now] her father's slave" (III.iv). Obedience to one's father seems therefore to be an absolute imperative, no matter what the cost, or what sort of father one has. What sort of father is Marcelo? To begin with, he is a revengeful father. Don Diego, the man Lisarda loves, is his enemy because he killed his son. However, rather than murder, the death of Marcelo's son appears to have been the result of an accident during a duel. Don Gil, an unbiased witness, declares that "that was an unlucky stroke of chance" (I.ii). Furthermore, Don Diego has already paid the penalty for his crime, as Don Gil again points out: "You served out a brief exile, for soft mercy still dwells in noble hearts, and they are quick to pardon" (I.ii). Don Diego himself is persuaded that he has also obtained Marcelo's forgiveness for his sin: "Heaven well knows that I am to blame for only one of those deaths, and he [Marcelo] already pardoned me for that" (III.iii). Yet Marcelo has not really forgiven or forgotten the offence done against him, as he reminds his daughter Lisarda: "You love and are loyal to a traitor, a murderer who deprived a son I begot of his sweet life? Isn't it your own blood he spilled?" (I.i). And when in the last act he has Don Diego in his power he does not hesitate to try to carry out his revenge. But perhaps the most dramatically telling scene in this respect occurs in Act I, when Don Diego comes to Marcelo's house to ask for both his forgiveness and his daughter's hand. The old man's reaction is, however, to demand a sword with which to kill his opponent, something for which Leonor reproves him (I.iv).

Can this passion for revenge, this hatred of Don Diego and later of Lisarda, when she dares to disobey him, be reconciled with the theme of obedience to one's father? The stern father who arranges his daughter's future without consulting her is normally a negative figure in Golden Age drama. A father who, like Marcelo, curses his daughter with the following words: "May it please God, my disobedient daughter, that you never marry, that you live in infamy, that you die poor, and that all despise you! May it please God that you end up as a fallen woman, that they call you a criminal, and that in all the world there be nothing as wicked as your life!" (I.i), must have been considered by the seventeenth-century audience to have overstepped both his authority and the bounds of reason.[68] Once again, it is Leonor, the dutiful daughter, that makes this clear when she observes that "those curses may encourage her to do the very things you fear" (I.i).

Spanish Golden Age drama teems with resolute and resourceful daughters who frustrate their fathers' plans and manage to marry the men of their choice. Lisarda differs from them in that, instead of using subterfuges, like the eponymous protagonist of Tirso de Molina's *Marta la piadosa*, she openly confronts her father. Marcelo, however, considers open rebellion against his authority an act of defiance against God himself. As he tells the disguised Lisarda in Act II, "she [Lisarda] has married against my wishes this very day [. . .] she has married him [Don Diego] against God's command" (II.i). We should not, however, take it for granted that Marcelo's *sequitur* ("she married against my wishes, therefore she married against God's command") was shared by every member of the audience. The problem is that Marcelo has a tendency to see his wishes as coinciding with those of the Almighty. The imagery used by Marcelo himself is designed to present himself as a God figure. For him, his daughters are his angels, as in the following exchange:

MARCELO: Angel, you are offending me.
LISARDA: If I am an angel, I cannot forget what I have once grasped.
MARCELO: It is that very grasping that condemns you. (I.i)

The suggestion that Marcelo detects a parallel between Lisarda's re-

bellion and that of some of the angels against their Creator is made
explicit in Act II, when he tells the disguised Lisarda: "Heaven gave
me two daughters; they were like angels, but the older one fell and
has now become a demon. This is the good angel that remains" (II.i).
Lisarda herself falls into the trap of casting her father in this role when,
after repenting, she returns to him like a sinner returns to God:

[MARCELO]:   I fear to buy you if you belong to God.
LISARDA: I will belong to Him if you buy me. (III.i)

Yet, there is an important contradiction in this scene that would
not have escaped a seventeenth-century spectator. For Lisarda appears
not only as a sinner returning to the fold but as a Christ figure as
well. Arsindo tells her that he considers himself "the Judas of your
innocence" and then sells her for "only thirty escudos" (III.i). She
herself stresses the analogy by remarking that "since that was the price
of a just man, it would be unjust to charge more for a sinner" (III.i).
Later, alone in her prison-tower, Lisarda regrets that Riselo did not
give her five thousand blows (III, iii), a reference to the five thousand
lashes that Christ was supposed to have received in the praetorium.
Without wishing to push the analogy too far (although Lisarda could
in some degree be seen as the victim of the sins of others), it seems
clear that we should beware of accepting Marcelo's personal opinion
concerning his role as God's representative on earth at face value. No
seventeenth-century spectator could have missed the irony implicit in
these words of Marcelo's: "I will do mercy and justice by marrying
off a live daughter and avenging a dead one" (III.iv). In making justice
and revenge synonymous, Marcelo's words run counter not only to the
opinion of numerous moralists, and of a few Golden Age characters,
such as Pedro Crespo in Calderón's *El alcalde de Zalamea*, but of the
Bible itself.[69]

With his passion for revenge, his concern for his own authority
and his disregard for the wishes of his daughters, Marcelo can hardly
be seen as a just and reasonable father. In the opinion of Don Diego, a
far more sympathetic character to a seventeenth-century audience, his
punishment may be nothing less than God's punishment, as he tells
Marcelo himself: "You are your own worst enemy. It is you who
killed her [Lisarda] rather than marry her to me; for heaven chose to
make you the minister of your own punishment" (III.i). As we can
see, obedience to one's father has turned out to be a rather problematic
aspect of the general theme of obedience to a superior power. So, of

course, is obedience to King and God.

Obedience to one's sovereign is the least developed aspect of this general theme. Relegated to the subplot, it is exemplified by the actions of Don Sancho, who yields Leonor, the woman he loves, to the Prince of Portugal. At one point, Don Sancho spells out the implications for both him and society at large of the Prince's marrying of Leonor: "Why do you want to strip me of my glory, my nobility, my very being? If this is a joke, it's gone far enough. If it is love, you must control yourself. You know that I know who you are. If you marry her, you'll marry beneath yourself. She is my equal; let me have her" (III.iv). Shortly afterwards, however, he accepts the inevitable: "And I, sire, must be the first to pledge my obedience to you. Forgive me, for it was love and jealousy that led my tongue astray" (III.iv). But what would have been the seventeenth-century audience's reaction to a Prince who rides roughshod over the feelings of a loyal subject and marries his social inferior? According to James Crapotta, "the code of honourable behavior demands that the noble *caballero* who finds his personal feelings at odds with the will of the King will cede to the authority of the monarch,"[70] as Don Sancho does here. But the fact is that in the vast majority of Golden Age plays where a conflict exists between monarch and subject, it is the monarch who at the end renounces the object of his desire. As José M. Díez Borque notes, "The King is superior to all the characters [. . .] because although he could satisfy his desires he restrains himself ("El Rey es superior a todos . . . porque *pudiendo* se vence").[71] By refusing to do what was expected of him, the Prince forces Don Sancho to give up the woman he loves. Can obedience to such a monarch be unambiguously endorsed by the action of the play?

But perhaps the most problematic aspect of the theme of submission to a superior power concerns obedience to God. Not because the Christian God may be presented as unjust or irresponsible or as making excessive demands on his creatures, but because of the difficulties characters seem to encounter in understanding and forming a significant relationship with Him.

Don Gil has throughout his life tried to be God's obedient servant, and to this end he has spent a life of "fasting and penitence, prayer and tender tears" (I.i). Yet, one single, unpremeditated act plunges him into an abyss of iniquity. Why? The answer seems to lie in the fact that Don Gil's idea of God is a purely cerebral one. He knows God with his intellect, not with his heart. Consequently, his relationship with Him fluctuates in accordance with a certain logical and ratiocinative process. To begin with, Don Gil's relationship with the Almighty appears to be a commercial and legalistic one. As he says to Don Diego, "God writes virtues and sins of all who live in this world in a book, and once that book is finished, He metes out rewards and punishments" (I.ii). Having committed a single transgression he believes that he has lost whatever credit he has managed to accumulate, as he explains to Lisarda: "You have lost much honor and I, much penitence" (I.iii), an idea he repeats later, adding "On your account I lost the wages I hoped to collect from the Lord of the universe" (I.iii).

But perhaps the clearest manifestation of his legalistic turn of mind is the way he argues himself into sin: "To be complete, a sin must have three parts: the thought, the consent and the action. Since that is so, I'm already halfway there. Prudence demands that one resists temptation at once. By hesitating, I almost gave my consent. Enough of this: I'm vanquished! God has let go of my hand. I can enjoy Lisarda without being recognized" (I.ii). The culmination of this attitude is found in the legal contract (couched in the highly artificial form of a sonnet) by means of which he sells his soul to the Devil (II.i).

It is not therefore surprising that this type of intellectual cogitating and hair-splitting should result in serious scruples. According to the New Catholic Dictionary, "to scruple [. . .] is to doubt about and hesitate doing something on false grounds of conscience [. . .] [scruples] arise from excessive servile fear in some persons, because they represent God as an exacting tyrant."[72] This is, of course, what makes Don Gil believe that God can abandon a saintly man like himself just because he has hesitated. His scrupulous nature combined with his commercial and legalistic way of thinking lead him inevitably to a belief in predestination. Belief in predestination is, after all, rather logical. It assumes that, guided by his infallible prescience of the future, God must have foreordained from eternity the events that occur in time, and thus must have destined all things beforehand to their appointed end. Angelio, with seemingly irrefutable logic, draws the practical implications of this belief when he tells Don Gil: "If you are predestined, you're sure to go to heaven. If not, isn't it insane to go through life without ever having fun?" (II.i).

Explaining his sudden change from saint to sinner, Don Gil expounds to the Prince his belief in predestination: "Many performed miracles but were later damned; and others, who had been great sinners, went on to perform miracles. There is no secure state in this world until death, for God alone knows who are the predestined" (III.ii). Whether one becomes a saint or a sinner, Don Gil seems to believe, depends entirely on the arbitrary will of God: "I lost God's grace. He let go of my hand, and hence in these mountains I capture, rob, rape and kill" (III.ii). But why does Don Gil believe that God has forsaken him? According to the Council of Trent, "no one in this life can without a special revelation know for certain whether he is among the predestined."[73] Don Gil, however, thinks he has received this special revelation through the phenomenon of kledonomancy, which, as A. H. Krappe defines it, is "the listening of stray words and their acceptance as *omina*."[74]

As C. E. Aníbal has suggested, the words Domingo utters in his sleep, as misunderstood by Don Gil, "may well be taken as a dramatic representation of the instinctive desire to sin."[75] However, because of his belief in a stern God and ultimately in predestination, Don Gil accepts them unquestioningly as evidence of his damnation:

DOMINGO: God's justice!
GIL: I can't escape it.
DOMINGO: Die, die!
GIL: It is God's justice that has come to threaten me.
DOMINGO: Don't miss this chance to enjoy her. I'll help you afterwards.
GIL: Now I feel better. But if I'm talking to myself, who can be answering me?
DOMINGO: Who but the devil himself?
GIL: Am I then damned?
DOMINGO: Yes, you are.
GIL: But if I'm damned, my penitence was in vain. (I.ii)

This unlikely dialogue serves to show that it is Don Gil's intellectual efforts to make sense of the words he overhears that leads to the misunderstanding. This misunderstanding has, however, deep psychological roots. The play's structure encourages the reader or spectator to conclude, not that Don Gil sins, as he claims, because he believes he is damned, but that he unconsciously wants to believe he is damned so as to remove the only barrier which separates him from the fulfillment of his repressed desire to sin. One outstanding feature of *The Devil's Slave* is precisely the way in which characters use logic and reason to talk themselves into giving free rein to their basest instincts and passions. Instead of reason controlling passions, Mira de Amescua has created a world in which reason is misused in order to justify indulgence in one's passions.

The Devil's Slave shows that logic, the power of reasoning, can be
a very dangerous weapon indeed. Logic is mostly responsible for the
many misunderstandings that occur in the play. Knowing that Lisarda
has written to Don Diego and seeing that she is no longer in her house,
Beatriz logically concludes that she has eloped with her lover. Hearing
that Marcelo has moved his household to the country, Marcelo's squire
logically assumes that Lisarda has also gone off with him. Noticing
that everyone in Marcelo's house is looking rather solemn, Fabio logically concludes that Lisarda is dead. He conveys this conclusion to
Don Diego who in turn logically assumes that "Marcelo must have
killed her to keep her from marrying me" (II.ii). Riselo has heard Don
Diego shouting "Be it known to all that one who hates Lisarda's blood
has killed her" (II.ii), and logically deduces that Don Diego, the family's enemy, has murdered her. Of course, the spectators know that all
these logical conclusions are wrong, and some of them may have even
remembered Aristotle's dictum that "the supreme good appears only to
the good man, for vice gives a twist to our minds, making us hold false
opinions about the principles of ethics."[76] This is clearly the case of
Marcelo. Thus, when he uses a series of analogies to draw a comparison between himself and God (both are fathers, both are justices, both
have good and bad angels, etc.), the audience should remember the
sort of man he is so as to examine more closely the terms of the comparison and perhaps note that its most striking aspects concern not the
similarities but the differences which exist between God and Marcelo,
especially as regards the latter's lack of compassion and mercy towards his enemies. Likewise, when Marcelo compares himself to Job,
the audience should be alerted to the fact that Job epitomizes patience
in adversity, unlike Marcelo who can only think of revenge.

The misuse of logic explains not only the many misunderstandings which occur in the play, but also Don Gil's sin and Lisarda's fall.
In Act I, scene i, Lisarda speciously argues that since she is a woman
and therefore without discernment, she is unable to overcome her dis-
like of Don Sancho and her love for Don Diego, thus justifying her
disobedience of her father. Her speech at the beginning of Act II also
seems persuasive at first sight. She claims that once launched in her
career of crime, she can not now turn back because "a dolphin cutting
the sea, a flaming comet, a horse in the midst of a race, a ship tossed
on the high seas, the swift course of a river, a lightning bolt that falls
from its sphere, an arrow shot from a bow: all these can turn back, but
not a woman, once she's made up her mind." This accumulation of

similes may be rhetorically powerful but can not hide the fact that the action of the play will eventually prove her wrong, for she does turn back and repent.

The Devil's Slave, then, appears to demonstrate, through the actions and words of the characters, that logic leads to either potentially tragic misunderstandings or to a reaffirmation of unconscious desires to sin. In this sense, logic can be seen as an important aspect of the equation appearance=evil detected by Roger Moore. In this play logic is in fact only the appearance of logic, having nothing in common with that science and art which, in St. Thomas Aquinas's definition, "directs the act of reason, by which man is able to proceed in the pursuit of truth without error, confusion or difficulty."[77] How then is one to find the path of righteousness and salvation? The Devil's Slave persuades us to believe that paradoxically this path is best found by following one's instincts and feelings.

The clearest examples of how instinctive actions can lead to conversion are provided by the main protagonists, Lisarda and Don Gil. When in Act II they, disguised as bandits, encounter Marcelo and Leonor in the mountains, Lisarda's first impulse is to kill them. Don Gil, however, persuades her to keep their jewels and to let them go free. It is at this point that Marcelo says to Lisarda that he finds consolation in thinking that he is more fortunate than her father "who begot a son only to see him become a highwayman" (II.i). Lisarda and the audience are, of course, aware of the dramatic irony implicit in Marcelo's words, but this hardly provides an explanation for the sudden change of heart which abruptly overcomes Lisarda, and which makes her kneel down and ask for her father's forgiveness. Remarking on the incongruousness of her act, Beatriz comments "Oh, what blessed thieves!" (II.i). Lisarda's action is clearly unpremeditated, intuitive, illogical, an instinctive reaction prompted by an overwhelming flow of sympathy for a father who does not realize that it is he who begot a daughter only to see her become a bandit. Unlike her other actions, this one is not preceded by any reasoning process. Afterwards, Lisarda attempts to explain it to Don Gil: "it does no harm to ask forgiveness so that I'll already have obtained it in case I decide to change my life" (II.i), but her words sound hollow. The real explanation must be sought elsewhere, especially since it is this action which (very much like Enrico's instinctive refusal to kill an old man in Tirso de Molina's El condenado por desconfiado) sets her on the path that will eventually lead to her salvation. Two other instinctive actions propel her along this path.

The first is her intuitive fear of the Devil, a fear for which she herself can find no explanation: "Where did this prodigious fear come from?" (II.i). The second occurs when Don Gil tells her to deny the Mother of God. Lisarda's refusal to do so is illogical, for she has already said that she is prepared to deny God twice if need be, and, as Don Gil points out, "isn't God greater than she?" (II.i).

Lisarda's impulsive actions are evidence of her basically good nature and show that her previous behavior is an aberration caused by the erroneous application of logic. Now Lisarda is prepared to receive the visit of grace, which, according to the New Catholic Dictionary, "in its widest meaning [. . .] signifies any gratuitous gift of God to a rational creature." One manifestation of grace consists "in a transitory help conferred for the performance of a good act."[78] This is the sort of help which Lisarda receives in Act II when instead of killing her ex-lover Don Diego, whom she has found tied to a tree, she forgives him. Initially the sight of the man who, she wrongly believes, betrayed her awakens in her a desire for revenge. As she herself poignantly puts it "I am a sailor who managed to swim out of the sea of sin, only to drown on the shore" (II.iii). Once more a simile with a certain poetic and intellectual appeal persuades her to indulge her passions. But then the gun with which she is about to kill Don Diego fails. Intuitively realizing the significance of this chance event, she tells Don Diego: "If flint itself can forgive you, I can soften my flinty heart. I beg your pardon, trusting that this will oblige God to forgive me too" (II.iii).

Without wishing to imply that *The Devil's Slave* had anything significant to contribute to the highly technical *De auxiliis* controversy which aroused so much debate from 1588, when Luis de Molina's *De concordia* was printed in Lisbon, until 1611, when the Inquisition forbade publication of any work on the doctrine of grace, Mira's play, composed before 1612, and concerned as it is with matters of grace, free will and predestination, could not but awaken memories of the recent polemic. As Daniel Rogers points out, the controversy aroused such widespread concern that when, in 1607, Pope Paul V pronounced that neither the Jesuit Luis de Molina nor the Dominican Domingo Báñez held heretical views, the people of Spain celebrated the announcement with fireworks and bullfights.[79]

In rather simplified form, Molinism attempted to reconcile grace and free will by teaching that grace derived its efficacy from free will, which, in its turn, was prepared and assisted by grace. In other words, that neither free will nor grace by itself suffices to attain salvation, since one could not operate without the other. In a poetic and dramatic fashion, *The Devil's Slave* may be seen to echo Molina's views in so far as it clearly shows that grace by itself does not serve to achieve salvation. The chance event which prevents Lisarda's murder of Don Diego leads to her repentance but does not guarantee her redemption from sin. She must earn this redemption by the exercise of her free will assisted by grace. In the words of the Council of Trent, "when God touches the heart of man through the inspiration of the Holy Spirit, man does not do nothing, for he receives that inspiration which he can also reject, but he cannot by his own free will without the grace of God move himself to justice before him."[80] This explains the soteriological necessity of her chance encounters with Lísida and Arsindo at the end of Act II. As Lisarda acknowledges, "God is giving me these temptations to move me to pity" (II.iii). But although these chance events can be seen as the visit of grace that is offering Lisarda the opportunity to perform good works, it is the exercise of her free will in giving up first her possessions (the box of jewels) and then herself (thereby becoming her father's slave) that eventually earns her salvation.

Don Gil's repentance charts a very similar path. As in the case of Lisarda, he will find salvation only through a series of unpremeditated, instinctive acts, by listening to his emotions rather than to his reason. His first impulsive act occurs in Act II, when, struck by the beauty of Leonor, he persuades Lisarda to spare the lives of her father and sister. He himself realizes that this request is illogical, when, in words which foreshadow what will actually happen to Lisarda's gun later on in the act, he says: "Don't strike that flint! [*To Leonor*] Calm down, lovely lady. What am I saying? A man who can't control himself is not rational" (II.i).[81] Whereas all of Don Gil's intellectual cogitating only led him to a belief in predestination and to a life of crime, this irrational feeling of love for Leonor will, paradoxically, lead to his salvation. Unlike his literary ancestor Doctor Faustus, Don Gil sells his soul to the Devil, not in exchange for power and knowledge, but to possess Leonor's body, the one thing that the Devil can not deliver. The dramatic discovery of the skeleton he has been embracing results in a typical *desengaño*, once again an instinctive reaction, unpreceded by any type of logical reasoning. In this scene Don Gil actually apostrophizes his feelings, rather than his reason, when he exclaims "Lost soul of mine, why are you so sad?" (III.ii).

Now that Don Gil has been transformed from an intellectual into an emotional human being, he can profit by the infusion of grace. It

seems as if, in the world of this play, divine grace can only descend
on characters who find themselves in a state of primitive innocence, in
close contact with their feelings and emotions. Very appropriately the
visit of grace takes, on this occasion, the form of a disembodied voice
which, unlike Domingo's voice in the kledonomancy scene, encourages
Don Gil to change his way of life. However, as in Lisarda's case, the
gift of grace by itself will not suffice to attain salvation. Don Gil
must exercise his free will and become God's slave in order to obtain
redemption from his sins. This he duly does in a moving speech in
Act III: "If you, Lord, are the potter, as the scripture tells us, I was
your vessel first, and though I smashed myself to pieces, I want to
return to your hands" (III.ii). This acceptance of responsibility on
the part of Don Gil (which contrasts with his initial rejection of total
responsibility for his fall: "God has let go of my hand" [I.ii]), together
with his affirmation of free will ("I *want* to return to your hands") make
possible the spectacular victory of the Angel over the Devil and the
recovery of the contract which Don Gil gave Angelio. Don Gil's final
speech in the play reiterates his will to do penance for the remainder
of his life: "And now St. Dominic's white robe and black cape await
me, for I want my penitence to astound the world" (III.iv).

* * *

In his *Drama and the Dramatic*, S. Dawson remarks that "literature
is concerned with concepts in an entirely different way from philosophy. In literature the concern with concepts is primarily ironic, for
irony is the mode of showing how the complexity of experience makes
necessary a continual re-examination of our conceptual language, to
check it, as it were, against the way things are, or may be."[82] In other
words, literature has a tendency to subvert philosophy . . . or theology, for with its insatiable curiosity to explore the dark side of our
conceptual language it will inevitably manage to turn any established
idea or belief upside down, just to see what the other side looks like.
With its peculiar rhetoric, literature will also attempt to persuade us,
at least until the play is over or the last page of the book has been
turned, to accept ideas which are not susceptible of demonstration in
the cold light of reason, but which contain a certain ineffable poetic
truth. The central poetic idea of *The Devil's Slave*—namely, that the
path to salvation may be found only instinctively and emotionally, that
the use of reason and logic may actually prove to be a hindrance in this
respect—runs counter to the Thomistic reliance on reason as an aid in

matters of faith and would probably have been rejected, not as heretical, but simply as misguided, by theologians in seventeenth-century Spain. This is probably the reason why Mira de Amescua decided that it was worth exploring in fiction.

J. M. Ruano de la Haza

NOTES TO THE INTRODUCTION

1 See Bruce W. Wardropper, "Las comedias religiosas de Calderón," *Actas del Congreso Internacional sobre Calderón y el teatro español del Siglo de Oro* (Madrid: CSIC, 1983), I, 185–98; and A. A. Parker, "Santos y bandoleros en el teatro español del Siglo de Oro," *Arbor*, 13 (1949), 395–416.

2 J. E. Varey and N. D. Shergold, *Teatros y comedias en Madrid: 1600–1650* (London: Tamesis, 1971), 169. (Hereafter abbreviated as *Fuentes III*). (My translation.)

3 See J. J. Allen, *The Reconstruction of a Spanish Golden Age Playhouse: the Corral del Príncipe, 1583–1650* (Gainesville: University Presses of Florida, 1983), 12–13.

4 Ibid., p. 45.

5 Juan de Zabaleta, *El día de fiesta por la mañana y por la tarde*, ed. Cristóbal Cuevas García (Madrid: Castalia, 1983), 310. (My translation.)

6 MS Res. 126, fol. 2 (Biblioteca Nacional of Madrid). The MS is signed by Fray Gabriel Téllez in Madrid on 8 March 1638. (My translation.)

7 Jean Sentaurens, *Seville et le théâtre* (Presses Universitaires de Bordeaux, 1984), I, 292. (My translation.)

8 Francisco de B. San Román, *Lope de Vega, los cómicos toledanos y el poeta sastre* (Madrid: Góngora, 1935), 126. (My translation.)

9 Sentaurens, *Seville et le théâtre*, I, 522. (My translation.)

10 *El día de fiesta*, 313. (My translation.)

11 J. E. Varey and N. D. Shergold, *Teatros y comedias en Madrid: 1666–1687* (London: Tamesis, 1974), 111–12. (My translation.)

12 J. E. Varey and N. D. Shergold, *Teatros y comedias en Madrid: 1688–1699* (London: Tamesis, 1979), 205–6. (My translation.)

13 Anon., *An Account of Spain* (London: Joseph Wilde, 1700). Quoted in J. E. Varey, "Cavemen in Calderón (and Some Cavewomen)," *Approaches to the Theater of Calderón*, ed. Michael D. McGaha (Washington D. C.: University Press of America, 1982), 232.

14 For more information about the staging of plays in seventeenth-century commercial theaters, see my two articles "La puesta en escena de *La mujer que manda en casa*," *Revista Canadiense de Estudios Hispánicos*, 10 (1986), 235–46, and "The Staging of Calderón's *La vida es sueño* and *La dama duende*," *Bulletin of Hispanic Studies*, 64 (1987), 51–63.

15 See, for example, the way the text of *Algvnas hazañas de las muchas de Don García Hurtado de Mendoça, Marqués de Cañete* (Madrid: Diego Flamenco, 1622) was divided among nine dramatists. The division of each of three acts of a play into three scenes or *cuadros* seems to have been very common.

16 See, for example, his article on "Cavemen in Calderón," note 13 above.

17 p. 52.

18 *Obras dramáticas completas*, ed. Blanca de los Ríos (Madrid: Aguilar, 1969), I, 1917. (Hereafter abbreviated as *ODC I*.)

19 *Obras escogidas*, ed. F. C. Sáinz de Robles (Madrid: Aguilar, 1974), III, 1036a.

20 *Obras dramáticas completas*, ed. Blanca de los Ríos (Madrid: Aguilar, 1968), III, 314a.

21 *Obras* (Madrid: Real Academia Española, 1926), II, 616a.

22 N. D. Shergold, "Juan de la Cueva and the Early Theatres of Seville," *Bulletin of Hispanic Studies*, 32 (1955), 1–7.

23 *A History of the Spanish Stage* (Oxford: Clarendon, 1967), p. 223.

24 Biblioteca Nacional of Madrid, MS 17.331.

25 An excellent study of music on the seventeenth-century stage is Louise K. Stein, "La plática de los dioses," in Pedro Calderón de la Barca, *La estatua de Prometeo*, ed. Margaret Rich Greer (Kassel: Reichenberger, 1986), 13–92.

26 *Drama and the Dramatic* (London: Methuen, 1970), 8.

27 Important work is, however, being done at present in this area, as evidenced by the recent International Seminar on "Actor y técnica de representación del teatro clásico español (del Siglo de Oro a hoy)" that took place in Madrid in May 1988, organized by José M. Díez Borque.

28 *Fuentes III*, 48. (My translation.)

29 *El día de fiesta*, 312–13. (My translation.)

30 Emilio Cotarelo y Mori, *Bibliografía de las controversias sobre la licitud del teatro en España* (Madrid: Revista de Archivos, 1904), 424a. (My translation.)

31 *Fuentes III*, 56. (My translation.)

32 *El día de fiesta*, 312–13. (My translation.)

33 Lope de Vega, *Acting is Believing*, trans. Michael D. McGaha (San Antonio: Trinity U. P., 1986), 69.

34 *ODC I*, 188a.

35 *ODC I*, 248a.

36 *ODC I*, 1483a.

37 *ODC I*, 1786a.

38 *Dramáticos contemporáneos de Lope de Vega*. Tomo segundo, ed. Ramón de Mesonero Romanos. Biblioteca de Autores Españoles, vol. 45 (Madrid: Atlas, 1951), pp. 217c and 231b.

39 *Obras*, II, 107b.

40 *Woman and Society in the Spanish Drama of the Golden Age* (Cambridge: Cambridge U. P., 1974), 118.

41 *Cours de Littérature Dramatique*, trans. Anne Necker de Sausure (Paris: Lacroix, 1865), II, 132–38.

42 *El Romanticismo español* (Madrid: Cátedra, 1982), 42–43. (My translation.)

43 See the edition prepared by Donald L. Shaw (Exeter Hispanic Texts, 1973).

44 *A History of the Romantic Movement in Spain* (Cambridge: Cambridge U. P., 1940).

45 *The Origins of the Romantic Movement in Spain* (Liverpool: Liverpool U. P., 1975), 164. (First edition: 1937).

46 *Romanticism* (London: Methuen, 1969), 55.

47 *The Aims of Poetic Drama* (London: Folcroft, 1971), 6.

48 Marius Schneider, *El origen musical de los animales símbolos en la mitología y la escultura antiguas* (Barcelona, 1946): quoted in J. E. Cirlot, *A Dictionary of Symbols*, trans. Jack Sage (London: Routledge and Kegan Paul, 1962), 10.

49 *Psychology and Alchemy*, trans. R. F. C. Hull (Princeton U. P., 1968), 131.

50 J. C. Cooper, *An Illustrated Encyclopdia of Traditional Symbols* (London: Thames and Hudson, 1968), 172–73.

51 *Psychology and Alchemy*, 190.

52 *La genèse de mythes* (Paris: Payot, 1952), 243.

53 C. G. Jung, *Psychology and Alchemy*, 96.

54 *Le symbolisme dans le mythologie grecque* (Paris: Payot, 1966), 75.

55 Ad de Vries, *Dictionary of Symbols and Imagery* (Amsterdam: North-Holland, 1974), 353–54.

56 Cirlot, *Dictionary*, sub voce.

57 *The Rope and Other Plays*, trans. E. F. Watling (Harmondsworth: Penguin, 1964), 89.

58 See Charles David Ley, *El gracioso en el teatro de la península: siglos XVI-XVII* (Madrid; Revista de Occidente, 1954).

59 See C. A. Jones, "Brecht y el drama del Siglo de Oro en España," *Segismundo*, 5–6 (1967), 39–54.

60 "Reflections on a New Definition of Baroque Drama," *Bulletin of Hispanic Studies*, 30 (1953), 151.

61 (México: De Andrea, 1957), 58. (My translation.)

62 (Barcelona: Vicens Vives, 1966), 322.

63 *Historia de la literatura española* (Madrid: Gredos, 1967), II, 337.

64 E. M. Wilson and Duncan Moir, *The Golden Age: Drama, 1492–1700* (London: Ernest Benn, 1971), 82–83.

65 "Principal and Secondary Plots in *El esclavo del demonio*," *Bulletin of the Comediantes*, 28 (1976), 49–52.

66 "Appearance (Evil) and Reality (Good) as Elements of Thematic Unity in Mira de Amescua's *El esclavo del demonio*," *Perspectivas de la Comedia*, II (1979), 79–80.

67 "Leonor's Role in *El esclavo del demonio*," *Revista Canadiense de Estudios Hispánicos*, 3 (1979), 284.

68 Curses and blessings are common in Mira de Amescua's plays. In *The Devil's Slave*, the specific items in both Marcelo's curse of Lisarda and his blessing of Leonor are fulfilled in the course of the play. In Act II, he specifically releases Lisarda from her curse and blesses her, wishing for her precisely the end that she will have at the play's conclusion. At the end of the play, Leonor becomes Queen of Portugal just as Marcelo had wished her at the beginning of Act I.

69 See Otis H. Green, *Spain and the Western Tradition* (Madison: University of Wisconsin Press, 1968), I, 18–19.

70 *Kingship and Tyranny in the Theater of Guillén de Castro* (London: Tamesis, 1984), 35.

71 *Sociología de la comedia española del siglo XVII* (Madrid: Cátedra, 1976), 81. (My translation.)

72 *The New Catholic Dictionary* (New York: Universal Knowledge Foundation, 1929), *sub voce*.

73 Don M. John Farrelly, *Predestination, Grace and Free Will* (Westminster, MA: The Newman Press, 1964), 142–43.

74 "Notes on the *voces del cielo*," *Romanic Review*, 17 (1926), 65.

75 "*Voces del cielo*: A Note on Mira de Amescua," *Romanic Review*, 16 (1925), 69.

76 Aristotle. *Ethics*, trans. J. A. K. Thomson (Harmondsworth: Penguin, 1955), 190.

77 See the entry for "logic" in *The New Catholic Dictionary*.

78 See the entry for "grace" in *The New Catholic Dictionary*.

79 In the Introduction to his critical edition of Tirso de Molina, *El condenado por desconfiado* (Oxford: Pergamon, 1974), 20.

80 Farrelly, *Predestination*, 141.

81 In the Spanish original Don Gil actually says "No dé lumbre el pedernal": see the edition of *El esclavo del demonio* prepared by James A. Castañeda (Madrid: Cátedra, 1980), l. 1270.

82 *Drama and the Dramatic*, 60.

FURTHER READING

Aníbal, C. E., *Antonio Mira de Amescua. I: "El arpa de David," Introduction and critical text. II: "Lisardo, his Pseudonym"* (Columbus, Ohio: Ohio State University, 1925).

Buchanan, Milton A., "Notes on the Spanish Drama: Lope, Mira de Amescua, and Moreto," *Modern Language Notes*, 20, no. 2 (1905), 38–41.

Carrasco, Rafael, *Lope de Vega y Mira de Amescua* (Guadix: Flores, 1935).

Castañeda, James A., *"El esclavo del demonio* y *Caer para levantar*: reflejos de dos ciclos," *Studia Hispanica in Honorem R. Lapesa* (Madrid: Gredos, 1974), II, 181–88.

——————. *Mira de Amescua* (New York: Twayne, 1977).

Castillo, Hernando de, *Primera parte de la historia general de Sancto Domingo y de su Orden de Predicadores* (Madrid: Francisco Sánchez, 1584).

Cotarelo y Mori, Emilio, *Mira de Amescua, y su teatro, estudio biográfico y crítico* (Madrid: Revista de Archivos, 1931).

Díaz de Escobar, Narciso, "Siluetas escénicas del pasado: autores dramáticos granadinos del siglo XVII: El doctor Mira de Amescua," *Revista del Centro de Estudios Históricos de Granada*, 1 (1911), 122–43.

Furst, Lilian R., *The Contour of European Romanticism* (London: Macmillan, 1979).

Green, Otis H., "The Literary Court of the Conde de Lemos at Naples, 1610–16," *Hispanic Review*, 1 (1933), 290–308.

Gregg, Karl C., "A Brief Biography of Antonio Mira de Amescua," *Bulletin of the Comediantes*, 26 (1974), 14–22.

Guillaume-Alonso, Araceli, "Les relations de parenté dans les *comedias de bandoleros*, au XVIIe siècle," *Autour des parentés en Espagne aux XVIe et XVIIe siècles. Histoire, mythe et Littérature*, études réunies et présentées par A. Redondo (Paris: Sorbonne, 1987), 193–212.

Huck, George Ann, "New Data—Mira de Amescua, Royal Chaplain," *Renaissance and Golden Age Essays in Honor of D. W. McPheeters*, ed. Bruno Damiani (Potomac: Scripta Humanistica, 1986), 130–33.

Jones, Sonia, "Two Cases of Kledonomancy in Lope's Theater," *Revista de Estudios Hispánicos* (Puerto Rico), 9 (1982), 137–42.

Mesonero Romanos, Ramón, "El teatro de Mira de Amescua," *Semanario pintoresco español* (1852), 82–83.

Mira de Amescua, A., *No hay dicha ni desdicha hasta la muerte*, ed. Vern Williamsen (Columbia: University of Missouri Press, 1970).

Parker, A. A., "Santos y bandoleros en el teatro español del Siglo de Oro," *Arbor*, 12, nos. 43–44 (1949), 395–416.

Rodríguez Marín, F., "Nuevos datos para las biografías de algunos escritores españoles de los siglos XVI y XVII: Mira de Amescua," *Boletín de la Real Academia Española*, 5 (1918), 321–32.

Romera-Navarro, M., "Las disfrazadas de varón en la comedia," *Hispanic*

Review, 2 (1934), 269–86.

Sanz, Fructuoso, "El doctor Antonio Mira de Amescua: nuevos datos para su biografía," *Boletín de la Real Academia Española*, 1 (1914), 551–72.

Tarrago, Torcuato, "El doctor Mira de Amescua," *La ilustración española y americana* (Madrid, 1888), 307.

Villegas, Alonso de, *Adición a la Tercera parte del "Flos Sanctorum"* (Huesca: Pérez de Valdivieso, 1588).

Zeitlin, M. A., *"El condenado por desconfiado* y *El esclavo del demonio,"* *Modern Language Forum*, 30, nos. 1–2 (1945), 1–5.

Antonio Mira de Amescua

The Devil's Slave

Translator's Note

The original text of *El esclavo del demonio* is of course written in poly-metric verse, but I have chosen to translate it in prose. The principal advantages of the verse form are the musicality of the rhythmic lan-guage (which, however, can also have a soporific effect) and the fact that it constantly reminds us that what we are reading or hearing is a stylized artistic creation, not a "slice of life." There is, however, little danger that anyone could achieve such a suspension of disbelief as to confuse this extravagantly unrealistic play, even in prose translation, with prosaic reality. The original play, though indeed in verse, hardly qualifies as poetry. It has moments of intense lyricism, to be sure—and I have attempted to convey the texture of those passages in rhetori-cally heightened prose, sometimes echoing the sonorous rhythms of the original—but the bulk of it is doggerel. To attempt an English equiv-alent would, I think, unnecessarily tax the patience of contemporary readers and audiences. Furthermore, 92% of *El esclavo del demonio* is written in octosyllabic verse, which in Spanish closely approximates the normal rhythms of prose. I do not believe it is possible to achieve such naturalness in modern English verse. The obvious choice, blank verse, has an innate gravity that simply cannot convey the varied tones of which Spanish octosyllabic verse is capable.

I have, however, found it necessary to resort to verse in translating the play's three sonnets and the songs in Act II. Unlike most of the other verse forms used in the play, the sonnet is highly intrusive and stands out in bold relief from the surrounding text. The songs, if they are to be set to music for performance, simply had to be in verse.

Michael McGaha
Pomona College

Characters

MARCELO, *an old man*
LISARDA and LEONOR, *his daughters*
DON DIEGO MENESES
DOMINGO, *Don Diego's lackey*
DON GIL
BEATRIZ, *Lisarda's maid*
DON SANCHO
FABIO, *his servant*
FLORINO

Marcelo's squire
ANGELIO, *a demon*
Two slaves
A musician
CONSTANCIO, *an old peasant*
THE PRINCE OF PORTUGAL
DON RODRIGO
LISIDA, *a shepherdess*
ARSINDO, *a peasant*
RISELO

ACT I

SCENE I

(Enter Marcelo, an old man, and his daughters Lisarda and Leonor.)

MARCELO: I am doing my duty as a father. Take my advice just this once, and show your gratitude by upholding this old frame, serving as columns to this edifice. If with sisterly love you let virtue guide your human actions, this old gray head will not envy your strong youth. My passage has been but a year: restless childhood, its May; youth, its summer; autumn, the perfect age; decrepitude, its cold winter. My body will hardly move. The longest life is short, since man is not eternal; and, since I'm in my winter, snow now covers my head. I spent the flower of my golden youth—the age you are reaching now—serving my king, and thus I enhanced the nobility I inherited. I mean to preserve it, and hence, Lisarda, I intend to give you the status you desire, for you two are the branches by which I must show my fruit.[1] Marry. Take your proper station in life. May God grant me this favor before time tumbles down this white wall, which even now is shaking. Don Sancho of Portugal, who has royal blood in his veins, is coming tomorrow to be your husband.

LISARDA: *[Aside]* That will be the death of me!

MARCELO: Leonor, you have offered your devotion to God eternal, a decision with which I am pleased. Now that you have chosen your state in life, choose a convent carefully. Your intention is holy, for in this life we are all pilgrims towards heaven,[2] though we travel along different paths. As you well know, every station in life is a path. Some are burdensome, others easy. The married woman bears a heavier cross, and the nun, a lighter one. All paths, however, lead to the innocent Lamb,[3] whom the different

realms serve with great reverence. I want my two daughters to
enjoy Him in these different ways. You two are my two arms. In
these two estates God will embrace you: He will hold one of you
close to Him, while embracing the other with the world at large.
With one of you as a nun and the other married, my house will be
honored, and I, on the threshhold of death, will have the strength
to weep for my past life.

LEONOR: My tongue will never dare say no to you.

LISARDA: [*Aside*] Love, I am mad with rage! I can't bear this any
longer!

LEONOR: I will be your slave.

LISARDA: And I, a disobedient daughter. Revenge and attraction are
effects of the soul,[4] which often twist the course of custom, dis-
course, honor, and reason. These passions are so powerful that
they tyrannize our inclinations. If not conquered, they give birth
to strange revolutions. I have been conquered by both, for I despise Don Sancho, and four months ago I surrendered my will to
your enemy Don Diego de Meneses. This is a strong inclination,
and I cannot conquer it. It has impressed itself upon my soul. I
have no discernment; I am a woman, and I've made up my mind.
If you marry me to Don Diego, I will obey you.

MARCELO: How can you speak so harshly to your father! You must
be blinded by love and I must bring you to your senses.

LISARDA: Father, I have no intention of changing my mind.

MARCELO: Angel, you are offending me.

LISARDA: If I am an angel, I cannot forget what I have once grasped.[5]

MARCELO: It is that very grasping that condemns you.

LISARDA: The power of the stars influences me.

MARCELO: A good woman cannot be forced.

LISARDA: Reason cannot restrain a person who is driven by love.

MARCELO: You love and are loyal to a traitor, a murderer who deprived
a son I begot of his sweet life? Isn't it your own blood he spilled?
What beast, what irrational creature, what barbarian would do such
a thing? Today you seem like one of those bad women whose love
thrives on abuse. May it please God, my disobedient daughter,
that you never marry, that you live in infamy, that you die poor,
and that all despise you! May it please God that you end up as
a fallen woman, that they call you a criminal, and that in all the
world there be nothing as wicked as your life!

LEONOR: Temper your anger, sir, for your curses are frightening.

MARCELO: This has uncovered my wrath.

LISARDA: And also my true inclinations.

MARCELO: Towards whom, you faithless child?

LISARDA: Towards my love.

(*Exit Lisarda.*)

MARCELO: Such shamelessness can only portend dishonor, for when a woman loses her shame, her reputation and honor begin to die. A daughter who scorns her own father deserves to live and die in infamy; like a crazy fool, she must follow in the footsteps of Flora and Lamia of old, not those of Penelope and Lucretia.[6]

LEONOR: Sir . . . No, I will not call you sir, for that title implies the rigor of unequal rank. I'll call you father, a name more full of sweetness and love. Temper your anger, for those curses may encourage her to do the very things you fear. Show her instead a kindly face, because once a woman has made up her mind, soft counsel is better than churlish chastisement. I will plead with her; and in the meantime you speak to Don Gil, that holy man whom Coimbra reveres for his fasting and penitence, prayer and tender tears. Beg him to ask Don Diego to be satisfied with having cruelly slain my brother and not to demand as well your honor, which is the very life of noblemen.

MARCELO: You are my heaven that orders all things well; you are the rainbow that calms my face midst the storm of my tears and pain. It is right that I restrain my rage. Because of you I now see that no one in this world of grief is so unfortunate that he has no consolation. May it please God that your life be unlike that of your sister, and that this old man, already near death, yet be so lucky as to see you Queen of Portugal.

(*Exeunt Marcelo and Leonor.*)

SCENE II

(*Enter Don Diego.*)

DIEGO: Love, though I'm following in your footsteps, I know not what path to choose; for I have fallen in love with the daughter of a man who is my enemy. I fear, I resist, I go on. Prudence fears in vain; I resist with all my might; but love is like lightning that strikes hardest where it finds the most resistance. Leander swam the straits; Hero hurled herself into the water; Thisbe took her own life; Pyramus pierced his breast.[7] Who did these things? Love did them, for he conquers effortlessly. The coldest temperament, falling in love, burns; and love begets bravery in the heart of the coward. I must be bold and not fear. I must possess Lisarda, for she loves me well.

(Enter Domingo, a lackey, with a note.)

DOMINGO: As I was passing by, a woman gave me this.

DIEGO: It's still light; I'll read it. [*Reads*] "Don Diego, my soul is on fire with love for you. My father has arranged a marriage for me; but if love makes you bold, come to my house tonight and take me away with you." Heavens, congratulations are in order! I'm so lucky that I hardly knew my illness when I came upon the cure! Fortune, don't turn your wheel back now, since you've raised me right up to the sun. Domingo, bring a ladder—though it will be superfluous, since the favor she has shown me has given me wings.

DOMINGO: Don Gil is looking for you.

DIEGO: It's my bad luck that this holy and penitent man should come upon me now as I struggle with evil thoughts and with temptations of the flesh. He has shown me much friendship . . . He is strong and I am weak. . . .

(Enter Don Gil in a long monk's habit.)

GIL: Don Diego.

DIEGO: What do you want?

GIL: To see you and talk to you.

DIEGO: Say what's on your mind.

GIL: Listen. Admonitions, my friend, are bitter flattery that give sweet life to the soul but are poison to the ears. They are a light unto our actions. They are precious stones with which our friends, parents, and elders enrich and honor us. It is discreet to give them to those who seek and honor them, but it is madness to give them where they are not esteemed or taken. However, duty requires that we give them to our friends, and this is even more the case when the body's life is in danger and the soul's salvation is at stake. I am your friend. The same school taught us letters, albeit few. If my admonitions are wearisome to you, my intention is good. Forgive me. You well know the nobility of the ancient Noroña family, lords of Mora, luster of the Spanish nation. You well know that that house you spy on, watch, and adore belongs to this noble, rich, illustrious, generous family. You are the worthy equal of any majesty and pomp, for the Meneses have few equals; yet with your rigorous hand you cut short the tender life of that illustrious firstborn son whom parents and sisters mourn. That was an unlucky stroke of chance; there's no need to go into it now. Your sword struck first; you happened to be fortunate. You served out a brief exile, for soft mercy still dwells in noble hearts, and they are quick to pardon. Noblemen are like children; they are easily appeased, as long as the injuries and affronts do not affect their nobility. Attacks upon one's life are dangerous wounds, but only those directed against honor are incurable. Their wounds, in fine, have healed, but barely so; for an affront incites the soul, and memory incites to affront. If then this old man does not imitate the African lioness or the spotted tigress by taking revenge, how can you—you tiger, lion, asp, lynx, rhinoceros—not amend your life and control your wild desires? *Seek goodness and flee evil, for short is our stay in this vale; Death, hell, and heaven exist; God will surely prevail.*[8] If you look upon Lisarda and fancy her with lustful urges, you'll double the weighty offense you've already committed. There may be mercy for a first offense, but it is doubtful that further wrongdoing will get off so easily, for repeated offenses exhaust even God's love, once He is angered. An offender should be the more fearful when his misdeed is forgiven, for justice then cries out, invoking the wrath of God. Restrain your appetite, for it is a malicious beast, a runaway horse that will not stop until it feels the bit between its teeth. If you aspire to marriage, find another woman to court, for no peace is ever safe if it results from discord. Long enmities give way to peace, but it is short-lived; for the journey from hatred to love is difficult indeed. To reconcile enemies is to gild rotten wood or to paint with tempera, which is easily erased. Seek other, softer means if you want blessed peace. Don't erect columns of love on bases of affront. *Seek goodness and flee evil, for short is our stay in this vale. Death, hell, and heaven exist; God will surely prevail.*

DIEGO: You're preaching in the wilderness.[9] It's time for you to go home.

GIL: The evildoer hates the light and seeks the shadows. And now that night has fallen, bringing the darkness you prefer, you want me to leave you alone. May God deliver you from your deeds, may He correct your intentions, may He inspire you and dispose you, and may He never release you from his powerful hand.

(Exit Don Gil.)

DIEGO: Blessed art thou, who knowest not of amorous passion. You know not coldness and are blissfully ignorant of disdain and jealousy. Yet cursed are you as well, for you don't experience the joys of love, which casts its cunning net upon our eyes.

(Enter Domingo with the ladder.)

DOMINGO: I've brought the ladder, but I was scared the night patrol would catch me on the way.

DIEGO: I think I see someone on the balcony. Is that you, my Lisarda?

(Enter Lisarda on the balcony.)

LISARDA: Is that you, Don Diego?

DIEGO: It is I, my lady and mistress, I who idolize that face, lovely image of God; I who am willing to sacrifice for your sake the soul I have lost and the faith that's still my own.

LISARDA: I who receive that faith and repay it with my own, who has not feared, who loves, who is sane, who is mad, who dares all, who is yours, who awaits, and who adores you. Try to get up here now while love transforms me into a man,[10] so that you can take me away without anyone recognizing me. Wait for me in this room. I'll leave it unlighted, locked and empty.

DIEGO: I've brought a ladder.

LISARDA: Burglar, you're stealing my soul!

DIEGO: Lean it against the wall, Domingo, for I now want to ascend to Lisarda's heaven.

DOMINGO: You're plunging into a thousand perils.

DIEGO: 'Tis love that makes me bold.

DOMINGO: Well, these things scare me to death. Must I go up with you?

DIEGO: You remove the ladder when I get up there, then hide in the darkness of this street, but be careful not to fall asleep. Remember, Domingo, you snore when you sleep, and sometimes you shout out the things that happened to you during the day and disturb the sleep of others.

DOMINGO: I'd make a lousy crane;[11] I can't stay awake for an hour, for I'm a heavy sleeper.

DIEGO: Stay awake tonight; it's important.

(*Domingo falls asleep. Enter Don Gil with a lantern. He encounters Don Diego on the ladder.*)

GIL: Tonight I'm conquering a soul for heaven. But Don Diego is climbing into Marcelo's house. I fear great misfortune! Don Diego.

DIEGO: I fear I'll lose this heavenly woman. What do you want?

GIL: Where are you climbing, you rock thrown at the clouds that goes up only to come down? You Nimrod[12] who build towers to assault the heavenly honor of holy maidens, get down those haughty feet, moved by obscene desire. Get down from there, you carnivorous wolf, thief of the treasures of honor, you cowardly cad! Just what Moorish castle are you now the first to scale? God writes the virtues and sins of all who live in this world in a book, and once that book is finished, He metes out rewards and punishments. Your crimes will soon be punished, for they are so infinite that the pages where God has written them are already full. Marcelo is the tree that brought forth the fruit you covet. If, like a rude barbarian, you tear away the branches, the trunk will be stripped bare. Life and honor are the columns that uphold his house. Detain your arm; leave him a life to live, and an honor with which to live well. Though you stripped his son's youthful body of its soul; though without dishonor his blood stained your palms, don't shed now his honor, for honor is the blood of the soul. No one takes or asks for what he can't give back. Remember, you murderous ingrate, that you are no king to give honor, no God to give human life. Fear God, who is like a lioness that kills those who attack her cubs and spares those who leave them alone. He is a mother bird, and your evil deeds defy heaven, since you are a hawk that scales a nest where there are chicks whom God covers with his wings.[13] There is a fixed limit to sinning.[14] How do you know that you won't be damned by committing just one more sin? Come now, my gallant young man, pay attention to what I owe you: if I'm in God's grace, I'm giving you your due.

DIEGO: I will do penance again. Balcony railings, I'll not scale you now. Forgive me, Lisarda. Don Gil, you've made me a new man, for no ears can be deaf to the voice of God. Domingo, take this ladder. You who with holy zeal compared me to a hawk are indeed heaven's own hunter, and you have broken my wings.

(*Don Diego comes down the ladder and leaves.*)

GIL: Congratulate me, heavens, on this conquest! My victory is no small one; no less than a soul has surrendered to me! But what is this, vainglory? Why do you treat me like this? The ladder is still here declaring its intent. Oh, what a strange idea! Jesus, my soul is slipping, and my intellect is silent. Faith has fled from my heart, for occasion is the mother of crime. When appetite swells, temptation is great. Lisarda is waiting upstairs for the man whom she tenderly loves. Imagination, stop it! Lisarda is beautiful. Heart, who makes you cower? Beware, insane thought, for you are like a river, which begins as a little stream that is easily forded but eventually bears a great ship. By going up, I can enjoy . . . Oh, heavens! Have I given my consent to the means of sin? No, I'm just rambling. My desire summons me to the fray; reason forms a divine squadron. My fear is infinite. Appetite sounds the call to arms, and occasion is the field of battle. Run, Gil, save your reputation! Living or dead, you'll not escape! It is a good thing to suffer temptation; but if Christ has gone to the desert,[15] the battle is already underway. My conscience is oppressed. Reason is losing the battle. Slay that wicked thought! Alas, my soul, your life is in grave danger! But isn't this just raving? I'm going up there. What's stopping me, since up there I'll take my pleasure? But why am I doing this? I have my free will in my hands. I'll never have a chance like this again, and if I use it well, Don Diego, I'll sate my lust in the bed where you hoped to rejoice. To be complete, a sin must have three parts: the thought, the consent, and the action. Since that is so, I'm already halfway there. Prudence demands that one resist temptation at once. By hesitating, I almost gave my consent. Enough of this; I'm vanquished! God has let go of my hand. I can enjoy Lisarda without being recognized.

(*Don Gil goes up the ladder; Domingo awakens.*)

DOMINGO: I've had it! I fell asleep on foot like a rented mule, but I woke up just when Don Diego went up there. While he's putting out his fire and repenting and being sorry, I'll just get forty winks. He's inside now. I'll make the ground my mattress, for no cotton bed is as soft as a skin full of wine. No knightly Roland[16] dares sleep as soundly as I unless his stomach is fortified with this liquor. If you're kept awake by worries and you want to sleep, just drink.

(*Domingo removes the ladder and goes back to sleep.*)

GIL: This room is empty, locked, and dark. Lisarda is waiting for Marcelo to go to bed. Her beauty has filled me with such determination and driven me so mad that it's as if I were already touching her. Oh, love! If merely imagining you is so sweet, the pleasure of possession can't be less. I'm inflamed with a thousand thoughts. Lovers' quarrels and love notes always go hand in hand; the one implies the other. What I'm doing will discredit me; I'll lose my reputation. No, I'll go with the world and retain my good name. Heaven knows my good intentions. I'll go back down right now. But the ladder is not here.

(*Domingo talks in his sleep.*)

DOMINGO: Don't come down until you've had her.
GIL: Who is that shouting encouragement? I'm terrified. Woe is me! I can't go down the way I came up.
DOMINGO: Wait, wait!
GIL: I couldn't go down even if I wanted to. Did someone see me climb up here?
DOMINGO: God's justice!
GIL: I can't escape it.
DOMINGO: Die, die!
GIL: It is God's justice that has come to threaten me.
DOMINGO: Don't miss this chance to enjoy her. I'll help you afterwards.
GIL: Now I feel better. But if I'm talking to myself, who can be answering me?
DOMINGO: Who but the devil himself?
GIL: Am I then damned?
DOMINGO: Yes, you are.
GIL: But if I'm damned, my penitence was in vain. Is the sentence what I think?
DOMINGO: Drink, drink.
GIL: My hour has come?
DOMINGO: Eat and drink.
GIL: If my fasting has been in vain, I may as well eat now.
DOMINGO: To your health!

GIL: I'll do as you say, since the flesh incites me with this toast.
DOMINGO: Enjoy this delightful occasion.
GIL: And many more!

(*Don Gil goes inside. Domingo awakens, upset.*)

DOMINGO: Is that you, sir? Damn it, I fell asleep! Is it time? Isn't
that you? There's no one around. I was buried in sweet slum-
ber. At first I dreamt Don Diego was having a fight and was
coming down the ladder without enjoying Lisarda's favors. Then
I dreamt that we were joyfully celebrating the wedding, drinking
toasts with heavenly wine. But the Pleiades are running away,
the Great Bear has stopped in its tracks, the North Star no longer
touches its Dipper,[17] and Don Diego has not come out. I'm in
terrible danger in this street with a ladder. Can he still be inside?
Did he leave while I was sleeping? I can't decide; I don't know
what to do. If he's inside, he won't stay till daybreak. If he wants
to come down, he can easily jump from the window, because you
don't need a ladder to get down. I'd better just get out of this
street, especially since doors are opening in Marcelo's house and
two men have already come out, and there's still no sign of Don
Diego. I'm running for cover, for fear is beginning to go to my
head like wine.

(*Exit Domingo.*)

SCENE III

(*Enter Don Gil with Lisarda, who is dressed as a man.*)

LISARDA: You've hardly spoken a word, Don Diego. Now we're
alone. Don't be bashful or withdrawn.
GIL: Have forbearance. Don Diego is not the one who has possessed
you.
LISARDA: Who are you?
GIL: A man who has ascended to the very sphere of God. But I have
been like Icarus,[18] flying on a waxen faith, and I've fallen into
hell. I've been a second Peter, and you were Pilate's fire;[19] to
cuddle up to you today, like a fool and an ingrate I denied God,
and I've lost Him. A mere cock's crow made him go out and
weep with tender breast;[20] but I, damned as I am, have heard the
voice of hell itself and still have lost my faith. I am Don Gil.

LISARDA: Woe is me! And what about Don Diego?

GIL: He brought me to seduce you in order to offend your father once again.

LISARDA: So this is how my high hopes are fulfilled. But I'm only getting what I deserve. My dishonor and miseries increase. This is the fate of daughters who don't obey their fathers. Who could endure it with patience?

GIL: To our grave sorrow we have been equally imprudent. You have lost much honor and I, much penitence.

LISARDA: Let me return to my house before the new day dawns.

GIL: You'll do no such thing; we must go ahead. My soul was cold as snow before, and now it's a blazing inferno. The life within this breast will now rush swiftly forward on waves of pleasure and profit, for it has burst the dam that virtue had built for it. On your account I traded prudence for the depths of hell. I lost my abstinence from the flesh, my reputation in the world, and the penitence I had done for God. On your account I lost the wages I hoped to collect from the Lord of the universe, and now I've gone back to work for a master who pays very badly. I'll spend my time from now on performing dastardly deeds, for this is how those who once were good but then turned to vice end up becoming unhinged. My lovely Lisarda, you must go with me. The world will be unable to deny us anything, since the powerful hand of God has let go of us.

LISARDA: What say you, my soul? "You could hardly fall deeper into disgrace." And you, my body? "Don't stay here, for you fear the convent's narrow walls." What answer you, my soul? "What's all this fuss about good conscience?" And you, my body? "Why do penance sooner when you can always do it later?" My father's curse is fulfilled. I fear heaven. I weep for my lost honor. The wretchedness of my life has reached its lowest point. Heaven, contributing abundantly to my downfall, gave me three enemies: Don Diego, who deceived me; my father, who cursed me; and Don Gil, who raped me. My father was blinded by rage; Don Gil was vanquished by lust; only the ingrate Don Diego has no excuse at all. Don Gil, will you help me avenge this affront?

GIL: In asking and forgiving she moves her fiery lips like fine sea coral. Follow the inclination of your star. I shall be a runaway horse, unstoppable in my headlong career of sin. Do as you please, take revenge. This soul of mine that no longer harbors faith, charity, or hope will carry out your orders exactly as you give them.

LISARDA: Goodbye, home where I was born! Goodbye, honor too soon lost! Goodbye, father I've offended! Goodbye, beloved sister! Goodbye, God whom I've lost! I'm lost. It's only right that disobedient daughters should have such misfortune.

GIL: No good soul is safe unless it flees the occasion of sin. I did not trust in God but relied upon my own strength when in danger. That was angelic pride, and hence God has cast me down.

(Exeunt Don Gil and Lisarda.)

SCENE IV

(Enter Marcelo and Leonor.)

MARCELO: Leonor, the heavy care befitting an aged father who has two unmarried daughters has afflicted me and kept me awake all night. If cruel Lisarda persists in turning away from my love, you will no longer be able to become a nun.

LEONOR: Your will is mine.

(Enter Beatriz, a maid.)

BEATRIZ: Sir!

MARCELO: Your fear frightens me.

BEATRIZ: My feet are frozen and stuck to the floor, a great pain smothers my life, and my voice sticks in my throat.

MARCELO: Tell me, what has shocked you so?

BEATRIZ: Just think what it could be.

MARCELO: Out with it! Don't be upset. You're doling out the poisonous draught.

BEATRIZ: Lisarda . . . Lisarda has written . . .

MARCELO: She persists in her headstrong lust. Don't even mention her to me, for just by pronouncing her name, you've already told me her crime. But tell me: whom did she write?

BEATRIZ: Don Diego de Meneses.

MARCELO: What did she write to him?

BEATRIZ: She summoned him.

MARCELO: Hush!

BEATRIZ: And he . . .

MARCELO: Alas! Don't stop now. Tell me: what do you know?

BEATRIZ: . . . took her away with him.

MARCELO: You should have said it all at once, for I have drunk in little gulps the purge you've brought me for my infirm age. If it be God's will that my declared enemy offend me, I must be another Job.[21] He has robbed me of life and honor; he can have my money too. I am a soft, loving stork;[22] he is a snake, a harpy.[23] He destroyed my nest and stole away two of the three little children I had in it. My daughter, what enemy winds bent your honor to such infamous desires? Is it possible for noble blood to harbor such vile thoughts? But the peasant and the bad nobleman fall equally into sin, for the path of human wickedness is broad, and brocade and sackcloth must suffer the same stain.

LEONOR: Don't get your gray beard so wet, for your tears are oriental pearls.

MARCELO: I'm surprised you don't call them coral, since I'm weeping my life's blood. Woe is me! What good can I now hope for?

LEONOR: How do you feel?

MARCELO: I feel faint.

LEONOR: Let me hold you up in my arms.

MARCELO: Then I'll see green May right next to snowy February.

(*He faints in her arms. Enter Don Diego Meneses.*)

DIEGO: [*Aside*] Love, in my heart you know that I seek peace. Intercede for me. Temper my great pain, since I'm coming to seek a remedy by such gentle means. I've come to ask for Lisarda's hand before I burn in her flames; but, though love drives me on, I'm weighed down with so many affronts that my noble blood cowers within me. [*To Marcelo*] Sir, if my grave offenses live on in your noble breast, if you are not satisfied and do not mean to forgive them, here is the man who has done them and who seeks to compensate. Give me death; though it is prudent for noble and wise breasts to be armed with breastplates of patience, proof against all affronts. I confess my wrongdoing, and I'm sorry if I have offended your person; but if the offense ceases, imitate God, who pardons those who confess their guilt. Peace can still come from our past anger, as heaven indeed has shown, for sometimes it brings forth a great good from a great sin. I love Lisarda, I am not your enemy. Give her permission to marry me, sir, for I deserve your favor. If you do this, you will give me pleasure and demonstrate your own greatness. Do it; and may you live a hundred years, an eternity, to enjoy our peace.

MARCELO: Give me a knife or a broadsword! I will avenge this grave
insult, for my old age is an elephant[24] and has taken on new fury,
seeing this tiger before me.

DIEGO: Don't bring it. It doesn't matter, since my own sword is at
your feet. Curtail your anger, for it is a cowardly sword that
strikes a neck bowed in submission.

LEONOR: Sir, Lisarda must become Don Diego's wife, since he has
her in his house. You should therefore pretend to be pleased.
Wouldn't you rather have it said that you gave her to him as his
wife in order to seek peace than that he carried her off with him
to be his mistress? Congratulate him, then, and let it turn out as
it may.

MARCELO: Your advice cuts short my pain. Don Diego, Lisarda is
yours; arrange for a joyful wedding, but with a single condition:
she must never enter my house on pain of her father's curse. She
can follow her inclination and get married at your house.

DIEGO: Let me kiss your feet! All will be done as you wish, for your
kindness knows no bounds. The marriage will take place at my
house. I'm going to prepare the celebration, since Lisarda brings
me joy. Love, I give you a thousand thanks, for my father-in-law
is now my friend. Marcelo, I'm mad with delight!

(Exit Don Diego.)

MARCELO: My daughter, it is not right that I should be present when
that girl who just wants to offend me gets married against my
wishes. I therefore think that we should go to the village. If I'm
there, I won't have to see this wretched wedding or know how it
turns out.

LEONOR: Whatever you say pleases me.

MARCELO: You are loving, you are loyal!

*(Exit Marcelo. Leonor remains on stage. Enter Don Sancho
and his servant Fabio, dressed in traveling clothes.
Don Sancho is carrying a portrait.)*

SANCHO: Fabio, a man who gets married without first seeing his wife
will surely have little peace and love in his home. In these matters
it is fitting that there should be some attraction and that one should
consult one's taste before making a choice. Hence, since I mean to
get married, I want to see Lisarda first without being recognized.

I'll not even trust her portrait.

FABIO: What excuse will you give for your visit?

SANCHO: My desire will come up with something. Is that Lisarda I
see?

FABIO: If so, you're as good as married. She seems to have set you
on fire.

SANCHO: While Marcelo's still alive, it's hardly right that I should
knock at heaven's door and ask if he's at home. I don't want to
talk to him right now; anyway, I know his intentions well enough.
Instead I'll busy my tongue with praising what I behold. The sun
has never set eyes on a woman, or rather a star, as lovely and
graceful as this. Look here, Fabio, is that Lisarda? I suspect it's
someone else.

FABIO: She's nothing like the portrait.

SANCHO: Her eyes are sovereign!

FABIO: If the hands in the portrait were just different . . .

SANCHO: No man alive deserves her!

LEONOR: What you are looking at, sir, is unworthy of praise, and my
father is occupied. Tell me what is your will.

SANCHO: I will my joy that seeing you may not redound to my harm;
I will my free will to restrain my inclination; I will my body to
the good fortune I've had in looking upon that sun; I will my soul
to the heaven of that beauty; and I bequeath this thought to my
memory!

LEONOR: All that remains is to die, since you've already made your
will.

SANCHO: That too is already done, for the wound was swift and deeply
cut. Only the man who sees his death on seeing you is truly alive.
He who, beholding that beauty, takes leave of his senses, be they
little or great, is truly sane and rational, and he who does not is
mad.

LEONOR: What flattery might I not expect of a man who is both
Portuguese[25] and a courtier? Where are you from, my good sir?

SANCHO: Since I was coming from the royal city of Lisbon to Coimbra,
Don Sancho of Portugal asked me to see Marcelo for him, because
he was detained by a certain matter.

LEONOR: [Aside] I suspect that this is Don Sancho.

SANCHO: My heart is bursting out of my breast! Such a beautiful lady
cannot be Lisarda. Fabio, give me some good advice.

FABIO: Although she's the younger sister, ask for her hand. Don't worry about the dowry.

SANCHO: I can hardly do that without arousing suspicion.

FABIO: Build yourself towers of hope; don't be dismayed.

SANCHO: If Lisarda is as lovely as you, God has given Don Sancho good fortune.

LEONOR: [*Aside*] He'll wait for her in vain. —Sir, you are the first man who has ever called me lovely.

SANCHO: Then all must have paid homage tacitly. [*Aside*] Fabio, I'm dying! —Kind nature made you such an epitome of perfection that you are more to be adored than praised; and hence, the eyes that gaze on you shame the tongue into silence.

LEONOR: So I'm pretty then?

SANCHO: That very doubt shows that you're also wise. You are so gorgeous and perfect that you could get away with being a fool, and you're so intelligent that you could get away with being ugly.

(Enter Beatriz with a hat.)

BEATRIZ: My lady, take your hat and cape, for my master is awaiting you.

SANCHO: Love, do you aim your steely bow at me only that I may die?

LEONOR: We're going to a village. My father will see you later, you lovesick Portuguese.

SANCHO: Give me permission to see you.

LEONOR: Certainly not; I won't allow it.

(Exeunt Leonor and Beatriz.)

SANCHO: Then I'll just take it; my very boldness grants it. Alas, Fabio! This is Leonor, the one who is to be a nun.

FABIO: She didn't seem to mind your calling her beautiful and making love to her. Fear not; that one will never be a nun.

SANCHO: I must see her in the village.

FABIO: How?

SANCHO: I can disguise myself. My love will never allow me to court another.

FABIO: Then go out through this door, for a crowd is coming this way.

(Exeunt Fabio and Sancho. Enter Domingo,
Don Diego, and Florino.)

DIEGO: Who can those men have been?

FLORINO: Who? It must have been Lisarda's suitor.

DIEGO: I'm sure he's in a fine fettle. They left in such a hurry—they must have seen us. Run inside and tell them that I've come with my relatives and friends—witnesses to my great love—to claim my Lisarda, and that my coach is at the door. Tell Lisarda and Marcelo.

(Exit Domingo.)

I've never seen a more cheerful sky; it's raining joy and laughter. Even the heavenly spheres are congratulating me on this peace, this friendship, with light and serenity.

(Enter Domingo and a squire.)

DOMINGO: Sir, we're all washed up. This wedding was just a trick.

DIEGO: What?

DOMINGO: Marcelo has gone away.

DIEGO: My blood is freezing in my veins.

SQUIRE: He's taken the whole household to the village and left me here in charge of the house.

DIEGO: Can this be true? What about Lisarda?

SQUIRE: He must have taken her with him, of course. I didn't see her, but she must have gone with Leonor.

DIEGO: This will be the end of me! How fickle is old age! He'll either give me Lisarda or I'll finish what I started before. How right was the man who said that old age is just a second childhood! Who can trust an old man or a child? It's only because I showed him respect that she's not in my power now. But she will be my wife. I promise you, I'll steal her. I'll not respect his years.

FLORINO: His castle is strong.

DIEGO: Love has always known how to come up with tricks and deceits.

ACT II

SCENE I

*(Enter Don Gil and Lisarda, dressed
as highwaymen and armed with harquebuses.)*

GIL: You must be sorry now. I'm sure you'd like to turn back.

LISARDA: A dolphin cutting the sea, a flaming comet, a horse in the midst of a race, a ship tossed on the high seas, the course of a swift river, a lightning bolt that falls from its sphere, an arrow shot from a bow: all these can turn back, but not a woman, once she's made up her mind. Dolphin, horse, comet, river, arrow, lightning bolt, ship: all these is the woman who knows not how to be obedient and subject to man. Shame and precious honor, self-interest, fear, and power will not be able to stop her if she is aggrieved and jealous. I am insane with rage. I have neither shame, honor, nor fear; so how can I repent until I have avenged my affront? You should rather give me confidence. You were the instrument of the insults from which I suffer, so you must likewise be the instrument of my revenge. This is the slope of the mountain which is known as Las Cabezas. It supports a forest of green and dry oaks on its back. Here in a nearby valley, refreshing to the spirit, my father has a village where he comes in the summer. On the other side Don Diego owns a little woods where he often comes to hunt and relax.

GIL: Then it is here that you plan to take revenge?

LISARDA: Yes, for in this thick forest I'll dare to satisfy you with a happy and secure life. I'll be a savage tigress against that wary hunter, for he has stolen my honor, which was the cub I was caring for. I'll make a coin of fear and with it buy from the shepherds little climbing goats, fresh milk, and green fruit. The traveler who's sure to pass by, seeing the harquebus on my shoulder, will hand over his well-guarded money. We'll make strong walls of this mountain range. If you climb to the top, you'll see that its rugged peaks reach to the very clouds. When July unleashes its snow, snakes transformed into delicate silver descend to the valley below. With the summer's heat these mountains sweat so much that in the valley, among the cattails, they form a little river. There are two little streams where May brings icy water, and January, milky snow, and where I once saw the swift deer run. There is a cave of slate and different stones, lined with ivy and adorned with vines. I know this place like the palm of my hand, for I have been a huntress, and the fleet-footed doe has fled from me in vain. It is here that I want you to run that stony cold heart through, for he pretended to love me greatly so that you could possess my body. Here I must put him to death, for he has been the instrument of the insults I've suffered.

GIL: You're a strong woman!

LISARDA: I am indeed; so strong that the world will yet call me Semiramis[26] the Cruel. I plan to practice the art of killing on all who pass through this place.

GIL: I will follow your obsessions, for, blinded by my error, I have become a dropsical sinner,[27] ever thirsting for more sins. Just give the order and I'll commit adultery, I'll steal, I'll swear, kill, dishonor, I'll scale the convent walls. See how quickly you've taught me to sin in this place! Only yesterday I was at the altar celebrating Mass. Only yesterday, dissolved in weeping, I held God within my hands,[28] and today with inhuman acts I have hell itself in my breast.

LISARDA: People are coming.

GIL: Cover your face and hide among those boulders, crowned with the lentisk trees, still green in spite of October.

(They put on masks.)

LISARDA: They will die!

GIL: Unless there are enough of them to give us pause. They are women.

LISARDA: Their weeping will not move me to pity.

(Enter Marcelo and Leonor in traveling clothes, and Beatriz, with a little coffer.)

MARCELO: Let the coach take the long way on level ground. You, Leonor, go down this hill holding tightly to my hand.

LISARDA: That's my sister.

GIL: She's a sovereign angel.

LEONOR: It's an easy descent. I'm only sorry that you've tired yourself.

LISARDA: Today the world will behold the strangest act of defiance ever seen in a lost soul. I want to shed my own blood. Let them die, let both of them die, for such are the deeds of a woman without honor and without God! My sister will inherit my belongings. I am tormented by envy. I must kill her, for virtue offends me, and I despise a virtuous woman. Marcelo may have given me life, but with his impertinent curse he forced me into *this* life. A man who hates his own daughter can't truly have begotten her. He's no father to me, he's my enemy, and so he has come to die.

GIL: I like that outrageous idea, because it's such an extraordinary sin! Such a deed amazes even me. No one can equal a woman in zeal and piety; but when she decides to turn bad, she's worse than the worst of men!

(Lisarda aims her harquebus at them; Marcelo kneels.)

MARCELO: Stop, wait! It's not right that I should beg for mercy and pity for myself, for it's but little life you take from me. Such threats are of no consequence to me; you're killing an old man who was already knocking at death's door. If I give up my life at your hands, you're just saving me from misfortune, for I am the most unhappy man in Portugal today. I beg pity only for this daughter, who is a jewel with whom I escape fleeing from my house, which has become a new Troy, burning in misfortune. I hope you will pity her, for even the proud elephant softens its fierce breast when an innocent lamb appears before it.[29] Heaven gave me two daughters; they were like angels, but the older one fell and has now become a demon. This is the good angel that remains. She is full of virtues; no woman equals her. Since my misfortune has ordained that the bad one should survive, please don't kill the good one.

LISARDA: Envy makes me even more cruel.

GIL: Don't strike that flint! [*To Leonor*] Calm down, lovely lady. What am I saying? A man who can't control himself is not rational. Though I've seen you before, as a wise man I then loved only your soul, and that protected you from me. Now that I'm no longer myself and am losing my soul anyway, I want to lose it for you.

LEONOR: If it's a life that you want, I'll gladly pay that tribute, for it will be less harmful to cut the unripe fruit than the tree that bears it. You are cruel, I know not why. If you live the life of a bull, let my life serve as a cape. Tear it to shreds while the master and father I adore makes his escape. I've never offended you, sir. Let my father live, and let me die. If you are a wolf in savagery, then tear the lamb to pieces and leave the shepherd alive. Yet God has given us such great love for each other that none has ever equalled it; by killing one of us, you'll surely take both our lives.

GIL: Those eyes deserve a thousand victories and trophies. They are heavens that shed lustrous pearls, and my thirsty desire quaffs them deep in my soul. [*Aside*] For your sake, divine Leonor, I will commit another grave crime. The previous one was a mistake, but this one is a blind furor engendered by lust. I must kill Marcelo; but Lisarda may obstruct what my soul desires. I want them to go to the village, for there I intend to possess her.

BEATRIZ: Sir, I beg you for the sake of heaven to let us go our way in peace.

LISARDA: [*Aside*] If you hadn't served as Don Diego's procurer, I'd never have been lost. —Tell me, Don Gil: what shall we do?

GIL: Remedy our necessity with their jewels and give them their precious freedom, since they are your own flesh and blood.

LISARDA: Ransom your lives.

MARCELO: How?

LISARDA: By giving us gold.

MARCELO: Sir, in this leaden box there are jewels of great value.

(*He gives her the little coffer.*)

LISARDA: Since they are mine by right, I'm taking nothing from you.

MARCELO: I was saving these jewels for a daughter I had.

LISARDA: Where is she now?

MARCELO: She has married against my wishes this very day, which has been such a sad one for me. Fleeing from myself I have become a fugitive so as not to see that wretched marriage I mentioned, for my enemy's glory—the bridegroom is my enemy—torments me with envy. Since she has married him against God's own command, you, who have so consoled me, enjoy her jewels.

LISARDA: How have I consoled you?

MARCELO: By making me think that your father who begot a son only to see him become a highwayman can deem himself even more wretched than I.

LISARDA: [*Aside*] I could rob you of that consolation just by taking off this mask. —I grant you your freedom. Godspeed!

BEATRIZ: Blessed be He, for now I can breathe without fear.

GIL: Wait, you must give me your hand.

(*He takes Leonor by the hand.*)

LEONOR: My life is short. Does he want to cut it off?

GIL: Heaven willed to mix blood, milk, scarlet, and snow in these hands.

LEONOR: Oh, heavens! I'm trembling!

GIL: And I am set aflame by touching these sweet icicles! How little I've known of love, of favor, of jealousy! But now I'm learning at last that woman has a rare capacity to give man pleasure. Now I understand how kingdoms have been lost for her beauty.

LISARDA: You must come back!

MARCELO: What must come back is my tears.

LEONOR: Don Gil, you friend of God, save us from this peril!

GIL: Madam, you have certainly picked a fine saint to commend yourself to.

MARCELO: What do you want?

(*Lisarda kneels.*)

LISARDA: For you to forgive the harm I've done you; for you to speak to me kindly and sweetly; and for you to give me a father's blessing.

BEATRIZ: Oh, what blessed thieves!

MARCELO: Since you wisely ask an old man for his blessing: may God remove you from this life. May He pardon you and give you peace, as I now pardon you.

(*He blesses her. Exeunt Marcelo, Leonor, and Beatriz.*)

GIL: That was no blessing, and you were wrong to ask for it, for as long as the sinner enjoys his sinning, there's no better life to be had. Or have you repented?

LISARDA: I'm far from doing so, but it does no harm to ask forgiveness so that I'll already have obtained it in case I decide to change my life.

GIL: They think you are in Don Diego's hands.

LISARDA: He's as good as dead.

GIL: How's that?

LISARDA: Today I plan to set fire to his woods. When he hears about it, he'll come, and then I'll kill him.

GIL: You're a cruel highwayman indeed, since you don't even spare your own father!

LISARDA: I choose to imitate the fierce Amazons of old, not that Trojan Aeneas.[30]

(She opens the coffer; they see the jewels inside.)

GIL: What sort of jewels are they?

LISARDA: They're not little ones.

GIL: And what's that there?

LISARDA: It must be a miniature of my sister.

(She hands him the portrait.)

GIL: You're showing me the sun itself!

LISARDA: I'm going to hide the box among these rough boulders.

(Exit Lisarda with the coffer.)

GIL: Love, let my soul on fire live now with lively hope that you will give me the living woman, since today you've given me her portrait. My soul swoons to call itself yours, but how will I endure your rays if your shadow blinds me like this? Leonor, my breast is on fire. I must aspire to your heaven. I'll be a very plague to the honor of your house. I will enjoy the good that I see, since I've come to desire it. The action will condemn me no more than the desire.[31] If it is the intention and desire that condemn the sinner, I'll give my very soul to possess you, Leonor.

*(Enter the devil, dressed as a young gallant.
He uses the name of Angelio.)*

ANGELIO: I accept your offer.

GIL: [*Aside*] Just looking upon this man has robbed me of my courage. My lips and bones are cold; my hair and beard stand on end! What a strange fear I feel! My soul, who can shock you like this? Why should you fear a man when you don't fear God himself?

ANGELIO: Fear not, Don Gil; wait.

GIL: Who are you?

ANGELIO: I am your friend, although I was your enemy until yesterday.

GIL: Why is that?

ANGELIO: Because you are imitating me. I too was once in God's grace, but in an instant I fell, and I have never repented.

GIL: And your name is?

ANGELIO: Angelio. I can't get over how little you've indulged in gambling and womanizing. If you are predestined, you're sure to go to heaven. If not, isn't it insane to go through life without ever having fun? If you want to learn black magic, I can teach you, for I learned it in the cave of Toledo.[32] I gladly teach it to others, along with the knowledge of infinite vices, giving free rein to desire without letting conscience interfere. If you conjure up hell among sepulchers and bones, nights and dark shadows, future events will be revealed to you. In all four elements[33] you will see strange signs: in plants, animals, and the movements of the heavens. Your pleasure will be infinite. With a free and determined life, you'll plunge headlong down the path of your lust. Since you love Leonor, even though it's incest,[34] I'll arrange for you to possess her right away.

GIL: How did you know that I adore Leonor?

ANGELIO: When it comes to knowledge, not even the loftiest cherubim[35] exceed me.

GIL: I like your science well; I'll learn your lessons.

ANGELIO: Only if you abide by my conditions.

GIL: Which are?

ANGELIO: That you abandon God, sign in your own blood a contract promising to be my slave, and renounce your baptism.

GIL: [Aside] My soul—if there yet be a soul in my breast—today your hope of salvation is destroyed. He asks but little, since I've already done almost everything he asks. When I abandoned the good life, I lost my soul. Then what am I waiting for? I'm only giving up something I've already lost in order to find what I want. I've offended God with three conditions, so I've already taken three steps down the staircase to hell. Some displeasure may cause others to kill themselves or despair; what I'm doing, however, is despairing for the sake of pleasure. —I shall do as you command, but you must give me Leonor.

ANGELIO: Disciples, come here!

(*Enter two men dressed as slaves.*)

SLAVE 1: Sir.

ANGELIO: Draw blood from Don Gil's veins, for he is to become my slave.

GIL: I want to be your disciple.

ANGELIO: Don't worry; I'm good-natured.

> (*The two slaves take Don Gil away.*
> *Angelio remains. Enter Lisarda.*)

LISARDA: Beside a crystal stream, a diamond mirror of the sun, I've just robbed and killed two travelers. It was but a flash of lightning, a test of my wrathful fire; but killing Don Diego will be the real thing, the bolt itself. I wanted to test my valor. But how could I fail to be fearless towards others, since I've ceased to fear my own death? I am a huntress of men,[36] those beasts unworthy of a better name. Today I'll adorn these oaks with human remains. They'll be sylvan pillories, and people will soon be saying that now the oaks bear heads instead of acorns.

> (*She catches sight of the devil, who sticks his head out,*
> *and she says:*)

Jesus! Where did this prodigious fear come from? What's happened to my valor and arrogance? How can I fear a mere man, who is no monster or giant? I'm so frightened I can't take a step. I'll kill him.

> (*She aims her shotgun at him.*)

ANGELIO: Your precautions are useless. If I can't die, how can you kill me?

LISARDA: Did you see a man?

ANGELIO: I saw a man who will never be a man henceforth.

LISARDA: What will he be?

> (*Enter the slaves bringing out Don Gil, now a slave,*
> *with the brand "S" on his cheek.*)[37]

ANGELIO: Did he sign the contract?

SLAVE 1: Yes.

LISARDA: Who could see Don Gil like this without being shocked? What's this?

GIL: I am prepared to serve you.
ANGELIO: Read the document.

(*Don Gil reads from the paper.*)

GIL:
If you will teach me magic's subtle art,
which Catholics would call barbarity,
and I wax strong, full of temerity,
and for a day can win sweet Leonor's heart;
I, Don Gil Núñez, do solemnly impart
my oath, not fearing hell's severity,
to renounce baptism, heaven's sweet charity,
and defy God and faith as an upstart.
His holy name from my mind I erase
to be your slave henceforth forevermore.
The pleasures of this life I now embrace,
renouncing all title to the Church's store
of merit. I freely give up my place
in heaven, to which Christ's wounded side is door.

ANGELIO: Good for you! Let those hands now kill men, because your first lesson will be in human bodies. This cave will be our shelter. There, amidst black altars, you can weep for those you've slain, as the crocodile is wont to do.[38]

(*Exeunt Angelio and his slaves; Don Gil and Lisarda stay behind.*)

LISARDA: What manner of clothing is that?
GIL: Slave's attire, for I've exchanged my freedom for a certain mode of inquiry that I commend to you most highly. I'm learning necromancy; they're teaching me in this cave.
LISARDA: No small achievement that! I'll do likewise and learn it with you.
GIL: They do impose certain conditions.
LISARDA: If you were to pile volcanoes on me, I'd walk right through their flames!
GIL: You'll have to renounce God.
LISARDA: I'll do it twice if need be!
GIL: And the Mother of God as well.
LISARDA: I cannot agree to that.
GIL: Isn't God greater than she?
LISARDA: Yes, of course He's greater; but if I now renounce both, who will intercede for me if I later repent?

GIL: Learn it without fear from me; after all, I gave you life. I'm no demon, and I can't repent. [*Aside*] I'd love to give you death in your wild youth, but killing you would be a virtuous act, and I despise virtue.

LISARDA: I am blind and sinful, but I still hope to do penance, though my poor sick conscience insists there's no time like the present.

(Exit Lisarda.)

GIL: Wait! Come back and be newly inflamed with the rage that possessed you when I told you the half truths, half lies about Don Diego. I want to find new opportunities for our crimes, since I've found a master who has taught me how to sin.

(Exit Don Gil.)

SCENE II

(Enter Don Sancho and Fabio, dressed as peasants.)

FABIO: Won't he recognize you?

SANCHO: It's impossible, for Marcelo hasn't seen me in many years.

FABIO: And won't the villagers find it strange to see you here?

SANCHO: It doesn't matter. They'll think we live in the woods.

FABIO: What are you after?

SANCHO: The noble soul of Leonor, who has already stolen mine.

FABIO: Lisarda didn't come with her father.

SANCHO: So I understand, but I don't know the reason why; perhaps she's dead, perhaps married.

FABIO: It's one and the same. But everyone looks so sad that I suspect she's dead. I'll find out today.

(Enter Don Diego and Domingo, dressed as peasants.)

DIEGO: Hush, Domingo. I don't need your advice. My soul is burning with love for Lisarda.

DOMINGO: And what do you intend to do?

DIEGO: Kidnap her.

DOMINGO: You already had your chance to do that, and like an idiot, you left me sleeping and went home to bed yourself. Was it because you were scared?

DIEGO: I was trying to do the right thing. Make friends with these peasants. I'll mingle with them and hide from Marcelo while seeking an occasion to carry out my plan.

DOMINGO: [*To Fabio and Don Sancho*] The Lord preserve you!

FABIO: Indeed, for He's a good master and preserves us all.

DOMINGO: Have you seen the lord of this village?

FABIO: Yes, we have.

DOMINGO: And the ladies too?

FABIO: He only brought one of them, Leonor.

DOMINGO: And what about Lisarda?

FABIO: I think she's dead.

DOMINGO: God damn you! Is that any way to tell me? Did you hear that, sir?

DIEGO: I heard, and I believe it must be true. Marcelo must have killed her to keep her from marrying me. Cruel old man! Ah, wretched me!

DOMINGO: No one in the household knows me. I'll find out for sure. Hide quickly! They're coming to this meadow.

SANCHO: Here comes the heaven I want to cherish in my memory!

(*Enter Marcelo, wearing a great-coat, Leonor, Beatriz, and a musician.*)

MARCELO: I'm very grateful for your wish to cheer me up. Sing, while I enjoy the fresh air of this countryside.

MUSICIAN: Give ear, Lisarda, though you distant be
from these fair vales, and hearken unto me:
in cruelty you outstrip Anaxaréte,[39]
though even Daphne's[40] not your match for beauty.
Your loving shepherd's had a change of heart;
of your unkindness he'll no longer smart.
To fair Gerarda he now sings of love,
as perfect as the angels up above.

DOMINGO: Master Marcelo, I has to ax y'all why our purty Miss Lisarda hasn't come here with y'all.

MARCELO: Don't mention her, don't kill me! My eyes fill up with tears whenever I think of her.

DIEGO: [*Aside*] With blood, you mean! It's true! How great is my misfortune!

MUSICIAN: You gave him ample reason to forget you.
He wishes he had never even met you.

Gerarda understands when she's well mated.
Who'd not choose love instead of being hated?

SANCHO: My lady, give me license to speak to you while he's singing.

LEONOR: I know who you are, Don Sancho.

SANCHO: Love makes men bold.

MUSICIAN: It's only fair that lovers should repay
                   an ingrate who from night to break of day
                   scorns love's sweet offerings; she's truly earned
                   the hateful coldness that her shepherd's learned.

DIEGO: Ask him right out if she's dead.

DOMINGO: I have to ax y'all—don't get mad with me—is Lisarda dead?

MARCELO: In this house she is dead.

DOMINGO: Did you hear? He said she died in this house.

DIEGO: Oh, lovely martyr! Innocent life, noble soul! Old tyrant, bad father! I'll kill him and avenge her!

DOMINGO: If you're smart, you'll keep your mouth shut.

DIEGO: I'm mad with grief!

DOMINGO: Remember we're among cowardly peasants, and they outnumber us.

DIEGO: She's dead! Domingo, great is my woe!

DOMINGO: I'm just your hearer; but your bad luck makes me feel like a broken mirror!

(*Exeunt Don Diego and Domingo.*)

MUSICIAN: In Love's own garden in the afternoon
                   lies sweet Gerarda in a sated swoon.
                   Content she sleeps, while music at her side
                   The crystal waters of a stream provide.

SANCHO: I can't offend you by adoring you. You must know, Leonor, that it is not easy to conquer such an attraction.

LEONOR: My father may be offended. My honor may be offended. Look what you're doing, Don Sancho. Your talking to me while dressed like that could cause gossip.

(*Enter Constancio, a peasant.*)

CONSTANCIO: Sir, if the great misfortunes of your vassals grieve you, pity and remedy mine, for you will see that it's above the others. I was going up to the mountain streams with a couple of boys and my daughter, whose wedding was to be tomorrow afternoon.

Would I had never gone to those streams, for now others gush forth from my eyes and will continue to flow without ceasing as long as my frail life endures! Four thieves came out, as cruel as they were cowardly. They commit unheard-of outrages in these mountains. They kidnapped my Lisida. Well may the eyes that have seen such things bathe these old gray hairs with tears! The captain of that infamous gang is a slave. When he saw her, he fancied her. Would that his eyes had gone blind! When she saw she was being captured and raped, she cried out, though all in vain, like a little goat that bleats, craving the voice of its mother.

MARCELO: This story brings back all my pain! It's like what happened to me.

LEONOR: Those are the men who stole my jewels!

SANCHO: How could you have kept this from me? They dared rob you—you, who steal men's souls? I must go and seek them out on your behalf. I will oblige you with their death. Farmer, if you will gather up some people in the village, I'll go in search of the thieves. Have no fear that they'll get away!

LEONOR: Surely there'll be many to go with you.

CONSTANCIO: I'll help you too.

SANCHO: With your permission, my lady, I'll go now.

LEONOR: You do me a great favor. Who is that handsome farmer? He's not from around here.

FABIO: He's a wealthy man from the next village . . . and your lover.

(Exeunt the peasants.)

LEONOR: Enough of this. Go on singing that ballad; I liked it.

BEATRIZ: He might sing another tune that would please you.

PRINCE: [*Offstage*] I'll listen to that voice while they shoe the horses.

(The musician sings. Enter Don Sancho, Prince of Portugal, and Don Rodrigo, his servant, in traveling clothes.)

RODRIGO: This man is the lord of these vassals.

LEONOR: Sing some more.

RODRIGO: Sir.

PRINCE: I'm very sick.

RODRIGO: I'm sorry to hear Your Highness say so. What is the matter?

PRINCE: I'm lovesick. Have you ever seen a more serious face, a livelier, more perfect coloring, more signs of intelligence, a livelier and yet softer speech? I'm dying, but I'm not afraid. I've unwittingly played the snake,[41] for I didn't close my ears to the sounds of her enchantment.

BEATRIZ: Two strangers have been listening to the music.

LEONOR: And one of them has disturbed me so much that I can't think straight.

BEATRIZ: They must be on their way to Coimbra.

LEONOR: What a fine body! How noble he looks!

PRINCE: That voice was worth dying for!

(*Drumbeats. Enter as many peasants as possible; Don Sancho, dressed as a peasant captain; Fabio, as a lieutenant, etc.*)

SANCHO: March in unison.

RODRIGO: My friend, who's that lady's father?

SANCHO: That man there. His name is Marcelo de Noroña.

PRINCE: He's a relative of mine.

RODRIGO: And tell me: where are all these boys going so heavily armed?

CONSTANCIO: To catch some thieves.

PRINCE: The captain is not bad looking.

SANCHO: I've mustered the troops here. Give them your blessing.

LEONOR: May everything turn out well for you, and may heaven keep you, Sancho.

MARCELO: Your name is Sancho?

SANCHO: Sir, my first name is Sancho, my middle name's Pascual.

LEONOR: And "of Portugal" is your surname.

SANCHO: You mean "of Leonor." We take our names from our masters. I am yours, as my soul confesses, though this enterprise be not of Caesar or of Rome. I'm not setting out with great courage or with the standards of Greece to conquer the three parts of the world like a second Alexander. I'm going to recover stolen property, and all my courage comes from you. But why bother to search for other thieves when your eyes are here before me? [*Aside*] But on whom are they gazing with such rapt attention? Alas, jealous thoughts! They're gazing on the prince. Heavens, isn't that Don Sancho, Prince of Portugal? Leave me in peace with the pain I already suffer without murdering me with jealousy too. Where could he be going except to see the sun that dazzles me? How attentively he's watching her! And she is wrapped up in him. I can but suffer in silence. Oh, ingrate! I'm dying of jealousy. —What are you staring at?

LEONOR: A stranger always arouses one's curiosity. It's not fair for
you to call me an ingrate. What favors have I taken from you?

SANCHO: The ones I've asked for, and you have not given me.

LEONOR: If I've allowed you to love me, surely that was a favor
worthy of a courtier.

CONSTANCIO: Let's go, captain. It's late.

SANCHO: A fine thing! Now I'm reviewing jealousies as well as
peasants!

(Exeunt the members of the squadron.)

PRINCE: She deserves a better look. I'm not so weary now. Don
Rodrigo, tell them to take their time in shoeing the horses. Meanwhile, I'll try to shoo away this pain.

(Enter Riselo.)

RISELO: Forgive me for the bad news that I bring.

MARCELO: My ears are used to sorrow. What is it now?

RISELO: Lisarda is dead. There's no doubt that Don Diego killed her.

MARCELO: How do you know?

RISELO: Because he's been going all over the countryside shouting:
"Be it known to all that one who hates Lisarda's blood has killed
her." And like a madman he tells everyone: "Lisarda's dead;
Lisarda has now died."

MARCELO: He's the one who hates my blood. He killed my son and
kidnapped my daughter; instead of marrying her, he's killed her.
He's given her a tomb as bridal-chamber; and he's proclaiming it
to cause me grief. I've run out of patience. I'll go to the court
and complain of these offenses to the king.

PRINCE: I can remedy your misfortune. Who is the offender?

MARCELO: Grief makes me incoherent. Tell him our story, daughter,
for recounting one's misfortune always relieves the pain.

LEONOR: Who are you sir, that you can remedy misfortunes?

PRINCE: I am a courtier who can report the matter to the king himself.

LEONOR: [*Aside*] You've also managed to mitigate the grief my sister's
death has caused me.

BEATRIZ: And what brought you to these parts?

PRINCE: I was traveling posthaste to find Don Gil, a holy man who is
a canon in the Coimbra cathedral, so that I could ask him to pray
God to heal my father, who is in grave danger, and who is an
important person in this kingdom. This, madam, is the purpose of

my journey; but since I laid eyes on you, I cannot leave this place
with freedom nor with my soul, for you could kill Eros himself
with love.

LEONOR: Such flattery is hardly to be believed.

(*Enter Don Sancho, dressed as a peasant.*)

SANCHO: If Leonor has found out who was staring at her, my hope
and joy are finished, for she's sure to fall in love with him. My
soul is on fire!

LEONOR: Captain, what brings you back?

SANCHO: I've come to ask y'all to give us some token to wear to the
fight—a sash, a ribbon, or a scarf. Because it's yours, goldarnit,
it'll make us strong as a . . . whatchacallit . . . oak tree! Naw,
that's not tough enough. What I mean to say is, like rocks!

PRINCE: If even a rude peasant esteems and adores you so, how is it
possible, madam, for one who knows your true worth not to love
you? [*Aside*] No one has recognized me.

SANCHO: It's pretty weird for a courtier to make us peasants jealous.

PRINCE: You're jealous then?

SANCHO: As much as I'm in love.

PRINCE: And just how much is that?

SANCHO: Enough to kill me.

PRINCE: I'll help you out then. Madam, give him some token; let him
go happily into the fray.

SANCHO: Do what the boss man says.

LEONOR: You can put this sash around his neck if you like.

(*She takes off a sash and gives it to the prince.*)

SANCHO: What you've given me is more like an instrument of torture
than a love-token, since it comes from another man's hand.

PRINCE: Peasant, it's a fine sash.

SANCHO: And may it bring me good luck.

BEATRIZ: Wait among those branches, for you've given them something to fight about.

LEONOR: I've handled this badly. Enough, let's go.

(*Leonor and Beatriz withdraw behind the curtains.*)

PRINCE: I know that sash means a lot to you, so I'll give you this
diamond for it.

SANCHO: I'm very much in love. No treasure can equal it.

PRINCE: Don't be such a stubborn fool.

SANCHO: I'm no dummy, leastwise not when it comes to this.

PRINCE: Don't you realize that it was up to me whether to give it to
you or not? The owner told me to give it to you "if I liked," so if
I don't like, I have the right to keep it, whether you like it or not.

LEONOR: The stranger is courageous.

BEATRIZ: Now they'll have to fight. It's all your fault.

SANCHO: You asked for it for me.

PRINCE: Well, I don't want to give it to you. You're a fool.

SANCHO: I may be playing dumb, but I'm smarter than you think. I
have my reasons for not talking back.

LEONOR: Is he afraid of him or showing due respect?

BEATRIZ: Why should he respect him? He's scared, and he's backed
down. That's obvious.

SANCHO: [*Aside*] I'm lost! I can't make up my mind. If I give up
the sash, I'm losing a token of love. The prince is my master. I
would be crazy to offend him, but if I don't, he'll consider me
a coward. Shall I tell him who I am? No, love is stronger than
loyalty. I've never been so confused. With Leonor looking on, I
must either give up my love or give up my loyalty. —Here's how
we'll settle this. I still want that there sash, but I won't fight with
y'all, cause I don't want to get in trouble with yer lordship. But
if y'all wants to see how tough I really am, give it to that Jew[42]
bastard there, and I'll take it away from him.

RODRIGO: Let me have it, sir, so I can show that churlish wretch that
I'm no coward.

PRINCE: It isn't right.

RODRIGO: You'd be giving it to a gentleman.

SANCHO: Sir, sir, go ahead and give it to him.

PRINCE: You must not treat it roughly but rather prove its worth.

RODRIGO: Now I've got it. You see it here?

SANCHO: I swear to God, it'll take both of you to keep it away from
me.

(*Sancho and Rodrigo begin to wrestle.*)

LEONOR: How could I have been so thoughtless in this mad thing that
I've done?

SANCHO: I'll tear either that sash or your very life from your chest!

PRINCE: [*Aside*] Peasants have no such courage. This man must be a
gentleman, but I must find out who he is.

BEATRIZ: He's brave, he's really in love!

RODRIGO: This villager's the devil himself! You can have the sash.

SANCHO: And you can have your life.

BEATRIZ: Now he's got the sash in his hand.

SANCHO: I'm just taking back what's mine.

PRINCE: But I intend to have it. You'll have to test your mettle again with me.

SANCHO: Then with all due respect and loyalty I must become a martyr to my love and your high state. Sir, take the half of it. By doing this, I show you my true self. I now have only half a will, for the other half belongs to the owner of this scarf.

BEATRIZ: Don Sancho of Portugal!

LEONOR: He's shown him great respect. He must have recognized him, and he must be a very important person.

SANCHO: Next time you decide to bestow tokens, you ingrate, do it more prudently.

PRINCE: He outstrips me in courtesy, and she is killing me with love!

(Exeunt.)

SCENE III

(Don Gil and the slaves drag out Don Diego and Domingo, tied up and half-naked.)

DIEGO: You thief and bandit, noble slave, whoever you may be: why are you taking me captive? Wasn't it enough to steal my money and clothing?

DOMINGO: Illustrious slave, valiant captain of these ministers who emulate old Cacus:[43] what has poor Domingo ever done to offend you? Spare my life, even if I must go naked.

GIL: Tie them to those oak-trees.

DIEGO: I recall some words of that saintly Don Gil that were so powerful and effective that they moved my heart. I'll move this man with them. "Friend, if you find my admonitions wearisome, my intention is good. Forgive me, and remember that God breaks peace and grows angry with a man who offends his creatures. *Seek goodness and flee evil, for short is our stay in this vale; Death, heaven, and hell exist; God will surely prevail.*

GIL: *[Aside]* Those were the last words I uttered in life, for I am now dead.

DIEGO: There is a fixed limit to sinning. How do you know if only
one more sin is required to ensure your damnation? *Seek goodness
and flee evil, for short is our stay in this vale; Death, heaven and
hell exist; God will surely prevail.*

GIL: [*Aside*] I preached that doctrine once upon a time, and with it
I moved a Christian breast. But I am more obstinate, for I have
become a demon. They're tied up now. I'll look for Lisarda, so
she can kill them with her own hands.

(*Exeunt Don Gil and the slaves. Don Diego and Domingo
remain, tied up.*)

DIEGO: They've left us with our lives. Oh, holy words! After all,
those were the words of Don Gil.

DOMINGO: Untie me, sir, and then I'll untie you.

DIEGO: What are you saying, fool?

DOMINGO: I must be raving, since I'm close to death. I look like a
jet image of St. Sebastian.[44] All I'm missing is the arrows; God
grant that lack be not supplied!

(*Enter Lisarda.*)

LISARDA:

When I compare the fabric of this world
and human glory to heaven's ordered round,
I know no better image could be found
of that angelic pride to hell's depths hurled.
When I consider the span of God unfurled,
this raucous age falls silent like a sound
unuttered. Shadows and smoke surround
the ancient corpse in shrouds of nothing furled.
This world, this life, this joy, this vanity
in sum are but nothing, smoke, shadow, pain.
The soul alone endures; it must be saved.
Then how can a woman who claims Christianity
defy her God? Indeed it is insane,
when one could be forever free, to die enslaved.

DOMINGO: Gentle sir, if you have need of a rope, I'll be glad to be of
service. I have it right here. Come.

DIEGO: Have pity on us, sir! We are the victims of a strange tyranny.

DOMINGO: Don't stand on ceremony. Untie me first.

LISARDA: [*Aside*] This occasion of sin opposes my good intentions.

(She puts on the mask.)

DOMINGO: This one's a thief too, for he's putting on his mask.

LISARDA: [*Aside*] At last I've come to see my scourge within my power. Is it really Don Diego? Are these bonds meant to drag me back down to sin? I'll now turn back to darkness. I shall not repent. I was a candle that shone more brightly as it died. It is Don Diego. —Prepare to die, you ingrate! I am a sailor who managed to swim out of the sea of sin, only to drown on the shore. Die, you traitor!

(She aims at Don Diego and pulls the trigger, but the gun doesn't fire.)

DOMINGO: Holy God, come to our aid! She didn't fire her gun. Sancte Petre, ora pro nos.[45] Since there are no sainted lackeys, you'll have to rescue me from this fire. I'll call on a good old boy[46] saint: Help me, Saint Bubba![47]

DIEGO: Even the flint of your gun has spared my life. What will you gain by killing me?

LISARDA: If flint itself can forgive you, I can soften my flinty heart. I beg your pardon, trusting that this will oblige God to forgive me too. God Himself had terrible enemies, and He forgave them. That was a clearer demonstration of His divinity than any of His miracles or fasts. Since my heart knows how to do the hardest things in following God's glorious law, this one will be easy.

(She unties them.)

DIEGO: Who are you?

LISARDA: I could say that I'm the one you've persecuted most.

DIEGO: If you were the one I've offended most, then you'd have to be Lisarda; but you're not. I haven't offended you, for I've never seen you before.

LISARDA: Take this, for you're naked. Find someone who will sell you some clothes. Here, take it.

(She gives him a ring.)

DIEGO: I accept both my life and that gift as a favor from heaven. What do you require of me?

LISARDA: That you never again do anything to offend Marcelo.

DIEGO: I am your slave until death. I will do your honorable bidding.

DOMINGO: Am I perchance the just man upon whom the lot has fallen? Am I to die?

DIEGO: No.

DOMINGO: I think maybe I'm stuck to the tree.

(He unties him.)

DIEGO: I'm confused and in awe of this man who has done me so much good.

(Exeunt Diego and Domingo. Lisarda remains.)

LISARDA: Now, holy God, I'm determined to serve you until I die, even if all hell tries to stop me.

(Enter Lisida, a shepherdess, bareheaded.)

LISIDA: Give refuge to a poor woman who has escaped death and retained her honor at so great cost to her face. I'm out of breath, I'm exhausted. A slave captured me. From his behavior I'd say he's the devil's own slave. He tried to rape me and overpower my chaste intent, but I managed to defend myself by screaming and biting him. God knows I am not dishonored, but it grieves me terribly that the people of my village will suspect I've lost my honor. I am poor and unlucky. I have no money, no dowry; I've even lost my good looks, and people are sure to say that my virginity went the same way.

LISARDA: Your intentions are praiseworthy. To me you represent the confusion of all women, and my own confusion too. I'm so envious of you that I'd happily trade places. I found myself in the same peril, but I lacked courage and was vanquished. Still, I can bear this pain with joy, for if you have been a second Martha, I can be Mary Magdalene.[48] You offered your tears to heaven, and heaven will give you a dowry. It's not right that I should enjoy what only you deserve. I'm going to give you some jewels that I've hidden in a little box behind this boulder.

LISIDA: What a wonderful alms, what great faith!

(Lisarda takes out the coffer of jewelry from among the rocks.)

LISARDA: This box I'm showing you belonged to an honorable bride, but she lost her honor, and it needs another owner now. Take it. There is the path; you can now return home safely.

LISIDA: I must first kiss your feet in thanksgiving for such a rare favor.

(*Exit Lisida. Enter Arsindo, a peasant.*)

ARSINDO: Thieves, have you no respect for age or poverty?

LISARDA: God is giving me these temptations to move me to piety. What's wrong, good man?

ARSINDO: I'm coming back from the fair at Coimbra; but now I'm weeping for my little children's wretchedness. I sold a few cattle for thirty escudos,[49] and here a slave has come out and taken them from me.

LISARDA: How many children do you have?

ARSINDO: Two.

LISARDA: This is the alms I will give you: for the sake of God, I will sell myself for thirty escudos.[50] I have nothing else left to give you, but I will be your slave. You must brand me and sell me to the lord of this village. I was lost through disobedience, but I will be saved through obedience.

ARSINDO: Sir, who would dare do what you are saying?

LISARDA: My salvation depends upon it.

ARSINDO: If it will save your soul, I'll obey you.

LISARDA: Lord, henceforth I offer you my heart in slavery!

ACT III

SCENE I

(Enter Leonor and Beatriz.)

LEONOR: I admit that I was in danger of falling in love with that stranger.

BEATRIZ: You call love "danger"?

LEONOR: And rightly so, for the only truly good love is like that of God. The love of men is a creaturely love, which is sure to give rise to jealousy and care, dishonor, restlessness, and fleeting pleasures.

BEATRIZ: Here comes my master.

(Enter Marcelo.)

MARCELO: My daughter, my consolation in the tragic upheavals of this life: as I've said before, though your natural inclination is to be a nun, it is important that you marry now, especially since today your wretched, disobedient sister has departed this life. We're expecting Don Sancho, to whom I had arranged to marry her, any day now. You'll just have to inherit her husband, since you're inheriting this noble house. Don Sancho is a rich and noble man, and they say that he is intelligent and handsome.

LEONOR: I've always obeyed you. I agree with you completely, and I think Don Sancho will soon be here.

MARCELO: Who told you so?

LEONOR: It's just a hunch.

BEATRIZ: Here comes the company of peasants.

(Drumbeats. Enter the troop of peasants. They bring on Don Diego and Domingo as prisoners.)

SANCHO: We went to the mountains in search of thieves. We didn't catch the thieves, for they fled out of fear. However, sir, I bring you the lovely Lisarda's murderer. I heard about what happened on the road. Execute him yourself, or send him to the king. Avenge your affront. Don Diego's pretending to be mad, for it serves his purpose to lower himself like this.

MARCELO: Just as the bird returns to its nest, the young man to his first love, and the water to the angry sea, so the offender returns to the hands of the offended. It is said that wounds bleed anew in the presence of the murderer. This is just what's happening to me as I look at you, for you've taken two lives from me. My children are another self, and hence my blood now gushes forth, for you are the murderer who has killed me twice. Knave, give me my daughter now!

LEONOR: Ingrate, give me my sister!

BEATRIZ: Traitor, give me my mistress!

DIEGO: It is your tyrannous hand that must give me the woman my soul adores. Tell me: what Jewish Herod,[51] what Verginius,[52] what Darius,[53] what Manlius,[54] what Roman Brutus[55]—which of these with his own hand would have committed such a deranged act? You are your own worst enemy. It is you who killed her rather than marry her to me; for heaven chose to make you the minister of your own punishment.

MARCELO: Now he's feigning madness; but he mustn't think he'll win his freedom thus. He knows that if a criminal is mad, he must be merely imprisoned. But since Fortune's wheel has turned again, giving me this opportunity to avenge my children, your fate is sealed. You must die not to avenge those you've killed but to protect the one that remains; for, knowing what a tyrant you are, if I forgive you today, you'll surely return tomorrow to kill the other sister.

DIEGO: It's more likely, cruel man that you are, that if a nobleman desires her, you'll kill her right here in this village to break the marriage contract, just as you killed my Lisarda. When you saw your blood shed, instead of imitating the pelican,[56] which bleeds and mangles its own breast to give life to its children, you behaved like the owl, which hungrily devours its own young. May heaven tame you, you wild beast, you Atropos,[57] who dare sever the tender thread of life! Let me take revenge!

LEONOR: What a strange madness has overtaken him!

MARCELO: You see how he's pretending? These tricks won't set you free!

DOMINGO: It may anger you for me to say so, but you're the one who killed her. You told me so yourself.

MARCELO: Another madman! Shut them both up in that tower while I summon the king's justice.

DOMINGO: [*Aside*] Unless God comes to the rescue, Domingo, your days are numbered! Me and my big mouth!

LEONOR: With all your wordy madness, how can you deny that you killed my sister, since you're wearing her ring?[58]

MARCELO: How dare you glory in the spoils robbed from her corpse! What a vile thought! You only wore that ring to hurt me more. You'd like to pluck out my very eyes! This confirms his wickedness. Put him in chains. I think it is but charity to take a life devoid of virtue.

DIEGO: Come here, come here! Like a rabid dog, I'll tear you apart with my teeth!

SANCHO: He's just pretending to be violently insane.

MARCELO: That's no seizure; it's just another trick.

DOMINGO: If you're a dog, then I'm a bear. Let's defend ourselves, sir!

MARCELO: Since all traitors are cowardly, late will you defend yourself, for you're both a traitor and a coward.

DOMINGO: You talk like that to me?

SANCHO: Your harshness is justified. Tie him up tight.

DIEGO: You lowborn knaves! Don't you know that I deserve more respect at your hands?

MARCELO: Take them away.

DOMINGO: I feel like a corpse attacked by vultures. Damn your foolish love!

DIEGO: Tyrant, give me my wife!

MARCELO: Give me my daughter, traitor!

(They lead them away.)

SANCHO: Permit me to kiss your hand out of reverence and favor.

LEONOR: I'd gladly do so, but I wouldn't want you to share my hand and will with that stranger.

SANCHO: I gave him but half a favor, while you gave him the whole thing.

LEONOR: Speak to my father. Tell him who you are.

SANCHO:　Not until I know your true feelings.

LEONOR:　What are you afraid of?

SANCHO:　That stranger.

LEONOR:　You get angry, and he goes away!

(*Exeunt; Leonor and Marcelo remain. Enter the peasant Arsindo with Lisarda, dressed as a slave and with her face branded: "Slave of God."*)

ARSINDO:　I've never seen such cruelty!

LISARDA:　I didn't want to be recognized. What I chose to write on my face bears witness to the wrong I've done. In the few years that I've lived, I've been as wild and mad as a runaway horse; this writing rights that wrong, putting the bit firmly between my teeth.

ARSINDO:　No one will know you now, for you've branded yourself so cruelly that you've disfigured your face as death is wont to do.

LISARDA:　Go on up to him, then.

ARSINDO:　I will obey you.

LISARDA:　[*Aside*] Don't reveal my identity, oh God, and I will do penance!

ARSINDO:　You've made me into the Judas of your innocence.[59] [*To Marcelo*] My lord, I've become so poor from struggling to support my children on my income that I am now forced to sell this little slave. I'll sell him to you cheap, and you'll be pleased with the deal, for though he's excessively marred, he's neither a thief nor a runaway; he is humble and meek.

LEONOR:　His countenance bears the scars of someone's wickedness. Upon my life, he's grieved my soul!

MARCELO:　He must have done something to deserve the shape he's in.

ARSINDO:　He's not like that because he has been wicked, but rather, that he may not be wicked. I consider him a good man.

LEONOR:　Buy him, just to free him from those chains.

MARCELO:　Give him to me on credit.

ARSINDO:　He's too valuable for that.

MARCELO:　How much will you take for him then?

ARSINDO:　Only thirty escudos.

MARCELO:　What is your name?

LISARDA:　Sinner.

MARCELO:　That's a low self-estimate. Sinner, you must not be worth much.

LISARDA: Since that was the price of a just man, it would be unjust
to charge more for a sinner.

MARCELO: The little slave is wise.

LEONOR: Tell me: why did they write that on your face?

LISARDA: Because of the wrong I've done.

LEONOR: Have you been bad then?

LISARDA: Yes.

LEONOR: And now?

LISARDA: I promise no longer to be bad.

LEONOR: How can you be so sure?

LISARDA: Because I'll have a better master.

LEONOR: Have you ever run away?

LISARDA: Just once.

LEONOR: Have you ever been a thief?

LISARDA: Indeed I have.

LEONOR: Will you do it again?

LISARDA: Never!

LEONOR: He's humble, for he admits his crime to both of us.

MARCELO: What's that written on his face?

LEONOR: Get up. It says: "Slave of God."

MARCELO: You have a master who is infinite. I fear to buy you if you
belong to God.

LISARDA: I will belong to Him if you buy me.

MARCELO: Have you then belonged to someone else?

LISARDA: One who has lived as freely as I has certainly not been
God's slave.

LEONOR: What will you be able to do?

LISARDA: Suffer, obey, and keep silent.

MARCELO: Those are the three parts of life.

BEATRIZ: Do you know, perchance, how to draw water?

LISARDA: If necessary, I can draw it from my very eyes.

MARCELO: The little slave is mine. What are you doing?

LISARDA: Kissing your feet.

MARCELO: Rise up.

LISARDA: No, rather tread upon me.

LEONOR: What great humility!

BEATRIZ: Come to me later, Sinner.

(*Exeunt.*)

SCENE II

(Enter Don Gil and the two Slaves.)

GIL: On the flowery banks of these clear little streams, which lock the feet of these oak-trees in their crystal shackles, I think we should wait till the sun tempers its ardent rays, bordering the clouds with a pearly red glow.

SLAVE 1:   Are you tired?

GIL: It is the deeds of sin that wear me out, not the pleasure of committing them, for that gives me rest. I've killed three peasants, raped two women, robbed ten travelers, and I've learned two spells. I am indeed the disciple of a good teacher, and the slave of a good lord, who teaches me broad paths of life.

SLAVE 2:   Someone's coming.

GIL: Though I no longer need to steal, the habit born of so many actions is strong.

(Enter the Prince and Don Rodrigo.)

PRINCE: The horses can graze on these green carpets which serve the rustic shepherds as their drawing-rooms while with swift course the sun moves towards the west, lengthening shadows.

GIL: The heat is the least of your worries. Who are you?

PRINCE: Harmless travelers.

GIL: Where are you two coming from?

PRINCE: What business is it of yours?

GIL: I'm curious, indeed so curious that I'd rather be a slave who's in the know than an ignorant free man.

PRINCE: If you must know, I'll offer this brief account: In the city of Coimbra there lives a holy canon who is a chosen vessel, like another divine Paul.[60] His name is Don Gil Núñez de Atoguía. Attracted by the story of his life and miracles, I decided to come from Lisbon accompanied only by this servant to visit him. My purpose was devout, but it turned out badly; for when I got to Coimbra, I found the whole town weeping bitter tears. It seems that Don Gil has been taken up in a chariot of fire like another prophet Elijah,[61] or else has withdrawn from the world to practice a more severe penance. At any rate he's nowhere to be found. What a strange, adverse turn of events! I'm returning disconsolate to Lisbon, where I shall await word from him concerning what direction my devotion should now take.

GIL: If it's Don Gil you're looking for, you'll find him living an extraordinary life as a hermit among these high boulders.

PRINCE: Let me get down and kiss your hands in return for such good news! Tell me where he is, and in gratitude I'll give you this chain.

GIL: It's mine already.

PRINCE: What do you mean? It's mine.

GIL: It's the toll you must pay me for crossing this pass. Fear not, and pay attention while I recount the miracles of this saint of yours: he flees almighty heaven, renouncing holy baptism; he robs all who pass by and kills many of his victims; he lusts after women and rapes them.

PRINCE: Silence, you liar! Don't offend his sanctity.

GIL: It's him you're talking to. Be not deceived, for our faith teaches us that no one in this world is truly holy. Only God penetrates the hearts of men. Many were cast down by fortune: Pompey, Caesar, Marius, Claudius, Marcellus, Tarquin, Mithradates, Belisarius.[62] Fortune raised others up: Cyrus, Artaxerxes, Viriatus, Darius, Sulla, Tamerlane, Primislaus, and Cincinnatus.[63] Some fall and others rise from humble and high estates. The same thing occurs with saints if they are not truly sanctified. Some have great virtue at the beginning, but a single sin overcomes them; others who once were evil only later become just. We have rare examples of this in Solomon and in Origen;[64] both were wise, both were just, but in the end they fell into idolatry. Magdalen, Dimas,[65] Paul,[66] and many others are examples of the opposite kind. You shouldn't be surprised to see me thus cast down. Many performed miracles but were later damned; and others, who had been great sinners, went on to perform miracles. There is no secure state in this world until death, for God alone knows who are the predestined. One sin leads to many others, for sin is cowardly. By opening the door to a single sin, we bring down the highest edifice. I lost God's grace. He let go of my hand, and hence in these mountains I capture, rob, rape and kill. I don't want to be known as a saint. You must spread abroad this bitter truth. In token of your promise to do so, you will give me that chain and your horses.

PRINCE: Can this be true? Is this really Don Gil?

RODRIGO: He's nodding that he is.

PRINCE: What a strange turn of events! Look here, Don Gil.

GIL: Don't preach at me.

PRINCE: I'm confused and troubled.

GIL: Give me that chain or you'll die; and continue your journey on foot, for I need those horses.

PRINCE: Can this be true?

GIL: Be quiet!

PRINCE: I will. Don Rodrigo, am I dreaming?

RODRIGO: It's an extraordinary prodigy.

(Exeunt the Prince and Don Rodrigo.)

GIL: You're right about that, for an obstinate sinner is indeed a prodigy. Take the horses over among those boulders. Meanwhile, I will find respite from my sadness in the flowers of these meadows.

(Exeunt the slaves. Enter Angelio, who is the devil.)

ANGELIO: Don't be melancholy. Why bathe your face with tears? Am I not your master? What pains you, what do you lack? I'm a good master. I am lord of two worlds, and God Himself calls me a "great prince" in His church, thus acknowledging my power. From the region of fire up to the sphere of water,[67] my prodigal hand embraces the heart of the earth. My vision penetrates the avaricious entrails of the earth, pregnant with treasure and with dead men. If perchance this solitude saddens and wearies you and your appetitite desires intercourse with different people, don't repent. Let not those eyes that idolize me weep! I'll take you off to dwell in an extraordinary city. Let me paint it for you. I'll use my tongue as brush, my words as colors, and your ears will be my canvas. Don Gil, I could paint you the city where I was born, from which I was cast into exile for centuries and long ages. I'll not offer you that city, for it exceeds my talent. I'll offer you another one, a creature of my imagination. It has all the greatness of Paris; the houses of Saragossa; streets as clean and broad as those of Florence; the sky and the ground of Madrid; the fertile fields and orchards of Granada; the bulging warehouses of Seville; the clear streams of Játiva;[68] the gardens of Valencia; the schools of Salamanca; the views of Naples, which rejoice the heart and soul; Lisbon's wide river, which, when it pays its tribute to the sea, appears to offer battle more than tribute; the outskirts of rich Valladolid, where meadows, fields, mountains, and water variously delight the eyes; the government of Venice; the walls of Moscow. The only thing missing will be the churches of Rome's court. Hither, as in Castile, they will bring bulls from Jarama, and you'll see brave men jousting on Andalusian steeds. The banquets and balls will be Italian-style; the tournaments, like those of Flanders; the gambling, as in Germany; the wrestling, as in Africa; music from Portugal, gallant jousting from France. There'll be fights and races like those of ancient Greece, and in the public theaters you'll see Spanish plays. The ladies you encounter will talk like the Sevillians, but have the faces of Granadans, the wit of Toledans, and the shapely bodies of Aragonese. Their clothing and accessories will be in the modern style of the Court of Castile. Seville will give you bread, the rugged Alpujarra mountains will provide game and choice fruit, and Ribadavia[69] will give you wines. Extremadura will give you bacon, Laredo and Adra,[70] fish. If you prefer imports, Calabria will give you wine; Lycia,[71] fish; Lycea,[72] fruit; Boeotia,[73] bread; Arcadia,[74] meat; Phoenicia, savory fowl; Transylvania,[75] sweet honey. You won't lack for riches: Dalmatia[76] will give you gold; Epirus,[77] brocade and cloth; and Tyre,[78] purple and scarlet. Your wish is my command; my generosity knows no limits. Don't regret serving me, nor let your heart be troubled.

GIL: My lord and master, whose knowledge astonishes the whole world: I want no Platonic republics, fabricated on an ideal; I don't want the riches the world offers as tribute to the haughty majesties the people idolize. Here among these towering pines, which form rustic garlands for the rugged heads of the haughty montains, I study delightful sciences, and, at the cost of passersby, I enjoy varied pleasures with a happy, unbounded life. I rape virgins, I slay men, I deny God, I flee from His grace. If indeed pleasure incites me, hell holds no fear for me. I only want you to fulfill a generous promise you made me, which was a condition of the contract by which I sold myself. I love Leonor. I suffer, I am in pain, living with hopes that turn my every hour into centuries and long ages.

ANGELIO: As I am obliged to you, I came prepared for this. In spite of her virtue, I have conquered Leonor. I've brought her here from her house. At this very moment her feet are treading this mountain, giving envy to clean snow and finest scarlet. Turn now your eyes and gaze on the rare Phoenix of Arabia[79] and flaming planet that enlightens the fourth sphere.[80] Reverence now her beauty; idolize this image on whose altars it is right that you sacrifice your soul.

(Enter Leonor.)

Come, speak, enjoy, taste! Why are you shaking? Why are you
dismayed? Leonor is yours; don't be shocked. Enjoy, taste, come,
and speak.

GIL: Lovely mistress of the world, who tyrannize souls with your
beauty, now giving life, now killing: blessed be the hour of your
coming, guest of our mountains, prison of the wills of all who
see your face. You appear to be sad to serve as soul of these
mountains. You are your own messenger, for you are the sun that
holds itself aloof. You are silent, Leonor; answer me if my gifts
please you. I will show you a generous soul with open hands.
Come with me to this cave; your glory will do it honor. Give me
your hand. Is it possible that I shall possess this lady?

(Exeunt; Angelio remains.)

ANGELIO: The savage bull now storms into the ring;
                  he's like a cruel Fury straight from hell.
                  Men tremble in their boots. Knowing full well
                  the mortal danger, they haste away or spring
                  the fence. Now wounded, the angry bull will fling
                  huge chunks of marble, shattered like eggshell.
                  They throw stuffed dummies at his horns to quell
                  his rage. He paws the blood-stained ground,
                                              [bellowing.
                  I am a haughty beast. I spare no one.
                  I tore a third of the stars from heaven's host,[81]
                  banishing them to the bullring of this nation.
                  I have been wounded. I'll have revenge, I boast!
                  I cannot strike God, for He is on His throne.
                  I'll therefore punish man, His choice creation.

(Enter Don Gil, embracing a skeleton covered with a shawl.)

GIL: Divine Leonor, since I have deserved to enjoy these transports
of love, I must have light to enjoy the wonders of your body. It
is not right that such good fortune should be relished in that dark
cave, though if I were an eagle,[82] even there I could see those
rays given off by the sun of your beauty. Happy am I, to have
possessed such an angel. Jesus! What's this I see?

(He uncovers her, and the skeleton falls through
a trap door in the stage.)

ANGELIO: It seems to be a property of sin that men think it ugly after
they've committed it.

GIL: Infernal shade, strong vision, is this how you repay me for my
lost soul? But then all pleasures of this life end but in death. How
right that wise man was to call beauty uncertain, a flower of the
field, a good that's only loaned to us, a tomb full of bones covered
with a cloth of brocade![83] Did I not possess Leonor? Where is her
wondrous beauty? It withered fast away, for sin is fire, and beauty
is a flower. Lost soul of mine, why are you so sad? God gives the
real goods only to his friends. The world can only lend them, and
those the devil gives are but apparent. Doesn't this frighten you,
shock you, and bewilder? Examine these pleasures. See, they're
not only brief but false as well.

(A voice speaks from off stage.)

VOICE: Man, oh sinful man! Your life gives me pain. Change your
life!

GIL: Lord, you call this beast a man? You call this erring path a life?
I heard voices in the air. Surely it was God who spoke to me.
Save me, oh Lord, from myself, and I will seek you like another
Paul if I've hitherto denied you like Peter.

ANGELIO: Don Gil, what is the meaning of this?

GIL: You have deceived me.

ANGELIO: Not at all.

GIL: The events speak for themselves. I gave my immortal soul for
some sun-bleached bones. You promised me a woman, but you
gave me an illusion—mere smoke, shadow, nothing, death.

ANGELIO: And when have the joys of this life been otherwise? The
pleasures the world gives have no more existence than this. The
only difference is that you drew back the veil and looked sin in the
face. The world and the abyss have never given a true good. You
have therefore not been deceived. I've given you the same thing
I've always given others. The woman who is flushed with beauty
and constant health can only count on a tiny moment of life, and
that moment is the present. Since that is the way things are, I
could just as well say her glory is fleeting the moment before she
dies as the moment after her death. You are my slave, I have a

binding contract. In your tomb you will see just whose slave you really were. Now behold my true appearance!

(Angelio steps onto a revolving stage machine, which takes him
out of sight, replacing him with the figure of a devil.
Skyrockets and guns are fired.)

GIL: Holy God, I rightly fear the punishment of my madness. You are God supreme, beauty extreme, but I left you for the opposite extreme. When I belonged to you, I was truly free; belonging to him, I am captive. In the vision he has shown me, I've not only seen that "I'm a slave, but whose slave" I truly am. He attempted to be your equal and now, though he is fallen, he's tried it once again, proving that his sin is mortal, for he has not repented. He showed this aspect, hoping that in my fear I would say he has the power of God, but though I am frightened indeed, "I'll never say" such a thing. I shall deny his power, for he obtains it only from you. When I abandoned you, I never gave up hope, although I have denied faith. I have also lacked charity. Belonging to such an owner, I have done wicked deeds, for I've done everything "my master commanded me." If you, Lord, are the potter, as the scripture tells us,[84] I was your vessel first, and though I smashed myself to pieces, I want to return to your hands. Make me your vessel again, for I'm fleeing from this master, because he's so wicked and ugly that it's irresistible "not to say that I'm his."[85] I have good reason to fear myself, for when I was on my own, with wicked zeal I denied God, the Virgin, baptism, the faith, the church, the saints, and heaven. I have no intercessor left. God's anger terrifies me. Who can help me now? The only one I have not renounced is my guardian angel. Let him intercede.

(He kneels.)

Ye angels, whose beauty no human creature has attained, you are strong to conquer. Rescue me! Take me from this slavery! Erase that contract!

(The vision of the devil disappears. Trumpets sound.
An angel and the devil fight, suspended above
the stage on machines; then they vanish.)

My eyes fill up with tears of joy, for the good and evil angels are fighting another battle for me in the sky. You choir of lovely

virtues, I know you'll vanquish him, for this won't be the first
time that you've crushed the dragon that swept so many stars
from heaven with his tail!

(Enter an angel or two in triumph, to the sound of music,
with a piece of paper.)

ANGEL: Don Gil, you and I have both won. Take back your contract.
GIL: At last my true joy begins! I was the devil's slave, but now
I'm the slave of God. My soul joyfully adores Him, for though it
betrayed Him, He redeemed it twice: once on the cross and again
now. I shall eat this paper up, for it lowers me to hell. Get inside
my faithless breast, for if there's nothing else so evil, you'll be
well placed in there. Gil, since heaven's supreme omnipotence has
rescued you, be warned from now on. If your sin was amazing,
let your penance amaze even more.

(Exit Don Gil.)

SCENE III

(Enter Lisarda in chains, and Riselo, pushing her on stage.)

RISELO: Enough of your hypocrisy! You may have spent all night
praying, slave, but you'll be looking for something to steal before
daybreak. I'm locking you up in this tower for the remainder of
the night so you can't run away. Pray and whip yourself, you
dog! Get on inside, for that's the only way I'll be able to sleep in
peace. I'm going to check on Don Diego, though I'm sure he's
safe in here. Since Marcelo has put me in charge of the slave and
of this prison, it's only right that I should be cautious.

(Exit Riselo.)

LISARDA: Those blows have made me happy. Give me suffering at
once, my God. I only regret that he didn't hit me five thousand
times.[86] No one has recognized me, since the sun burned my face
so much while I was wandering in the mountains; or perchance it
is sin that has caused these defects in my face, for since my soul
changed, my appearance must have changed too.

(Enter Don Diego and Domingo in shackles.)

DIEGO: Day has already dawned!

DOMINGO: You couldn't prove it by me, for I have lost my sight in these dark caves. By God, I'm in Limbo,[87] like one with neither baptism nor sin.

DIEGO: But I am burning in my own hell!

DOMINGO: Well, at least we're neighbors then.

(Lisarda rattles her chains.)

Jesus, that was the noise of a chain!

DIEGO: What can it be?

DOMINGO: It must be the soul of Lisarda, wandering in pain. This must be where they killed her, and since she loved you so much, she was damned.

DIEGO: Alas!

DOMINGO: Those sighs are terrifying.

DIEGO: Don't talk so fast, calm down.

LISARDA: Oh, unfortunate Lisarda, what a judgment awaits you! What a terrible thing you did, Don Diego!

DOMINGO: Did you hear that?

DIEGO: It is she, and she's complaining of me.

LISARDA: Woe is me! Why did you treat me so badly? But you'll have to pay for it later.

DIEGO: Stop! My end is come. Marcelo will surely kill me, for she says that I must pay for having adored her.

DOMINGO: I can't stop shaking. I wish I were an exorcist!

LISARDA: Suffer in silence, sinner, until your body dies.

DIEGO: Domingo, am I really that wicked? Have I really sinned that much?

DOMINGO: Indeed you have, by involving me in this muddle.

DIEGO: Go back to the other room where we were before.

(In gesturing to Domingo, Don Diego rattles his chain.)

LISARDA: Oh God, what a strange sound! It surely portends further torment!

DIEGO: I'll speak to her. Lisarda, my innocence exonerates me; I'm not to blame for your misfortune.

LISARDA: That voice gives me chills. It sounds just like Don Diego. Can it be Don Diego?

DIEGO: On this occasion I hope for your forgiveness.

LISARDA: This sad soul offers it to you.

DIEGO: Your father has treated me thus cruelly.

LISARDA: [*Aside*] My father must have killed him to avenge the wrongs he did to both of us.

DIEGO: I am guiltless, for I could have carried you off to my house, but Don Gil Núñez de Atoguía took the opportunity from me.

LISARDA: Why did you bring him to leave me in dishonor?

DIEGO: On that last wretched night that you spoke to me, the night when you say that you were deceived and dishonored, I was climbing up to your balcony when he preached to me so convincingly that I changed my mind. To make a long story short, I took my leave. Would I had never left! Tell me what I can do for you, Lisarda, and let me go and get some rest.

LISARDA: We'll soon see one another in the afterlife.

DIEGO: Did you hear how she foretold my death? I can't control my emotions as I leave this place.

DOMINGO: You think you're in bad shape! I can't even control my bowels!

(*Exeunt Don Diego and Domingo; Lisarda remains on stage.*)

LISARDA: So Don Diego was innocent after all, but unlucky nonetheless, for they've killed him, and it was all my fault. Lord, they say that pain and care can kill. Let then the pain and suffering of sin kill me! Give me such true sorrow for having offended you that my very heart will melt in tears. Let me go blind from weeping, let me now die of pain!

(*Enter Riselo.*)

RISELO: Sinner, it's morning now. Get up and go to work in the fields.

LISARDA: Let's go, then, dear companion (I'm speaking to you, my dear chain).

RISELO: That dog can't seem to get a move on. Hey there, Don Diego de Meneses!

(*Exit Lisarda; enter Don Diego and Domingo.*)

DIEGO: Who calls me?

RISELO: Today you'll die.

DIEGO: I knew it before you said so.

RISELO: Prepare yourself then, for Marcelo wants to avenge his son and daughter.

DIEGO: Heaven well knows that I am to blame for only one of those deaths, and he already pardoned me for that.

DOMINGO: And may God forgive you, amen! Tell me, must poor, wretched Domingo die too?

RISELO: You'll both be put to death this very day![88]

DOMINGO: May God give you bad news to repay you for that piece of information!

(Exeunt.)

SCENE IV

(Enter the Prince and Don Rodrigo.)

PRINCE: Love brings me back to this village. Don't spoil my mood with your objections, Don Rodrigo.

RODRIGO: Do you mean to commit yourself to marriage and upset your father and the kingdom?

PRINCE: Since she's my cousin and her reputation is impeccable, what is wrong with my marrying her?

RODRIGO: You ought not to do it without the king's consent.

PRINCE: We can keep it secret till the proper time.

RODRIGO: Here comes Marcelo. Will you tell him who you are?

PRINCE: He might not dare let me marry his daughter out of fear of my father, so I've decided on another way.

(Enter Marcelo.)

May heaven keep you, illustrious and generous Marcelo! I've brought you a letter from Prince Sancho.

MARCELO: Welcome.

PRINCE: Do you know his highness' handwriting?

MARCELO: I've seen it often. [*He reads the letter.*] "My dear friend and relative: The bearer of this letter is Don Sancho. Treat him as you would myself, for I esteem him highly, and give him your daughter in marriage. You will never regret it. Signed, Prince Sancho." Are you Don Sancho of Portugal, sir?

PRINCE: Of that you can rest assured. [*Aside*] I am Don Sancho, and I'll be King of Portugal. —I was here once before, but I haven't come to speak to you till now.

MARCELO: You did me an injustice, and you underestimate me by arming yourself with that letter from the prince. I have been anxiously waiting to serve you in my house, where I hope to marry you to my daughter Leonor, since my older daughter, Lisarda, is dead.

PRINCE: I heard all about that.

MARCELO: I plan to punish her treacherous husband, for I am the lord of these lands and have legal authority here.

PRINCE: I am sure both the prince and the king will approve.

MARCELO: Go inside the house and rest, sir, while I tell Leonor of your arrival.

PRINCE: She is the angel I adore.

(Exeunt the Prince and Don Rodrigo.)

MARCELO: He clearly manifests his noble and illustrious birth, and the prince does us honor with his letter. Leonor, my daughter, Don Sancho has arrived.

(Enter Leonor and Beatriz.)

He's already seen you, for he came here in disguise. He's spoken to me now, and he wants to marry you right away. Make all the necessary arrangements.

LEONOR: I already knew of his arrival, sir. Doubtless he wanted to see me, and that's why he came in disguise.

MARCELO: An act befitting an intelligent man. Wait here. I'll bring him so that you can see him.

(Exit Marcelo. Leonor remains on stage.
Enter Don Sancho and Fabio.)

SANCHO: I've come back, Leonor. I've decided to tell your illustrious father who I am.

LEONOR: He already knows that you're in the village, and he wants us to be married.

SANCHO: Oh, lucky me!

LEONOR: Tell me: who was the man with whom you split my sash?

SANCHO: A scoundrel, an imposter who plays tricks on people, pretending to be a king, prince, or duke. [*Aside*] The prince has come back! I'm burning with jealousy!

LEONOR: Then why did you show him such respect?

SANCHO: I was afraid he might play some trick or reveal my true identity.

(Enter Marcelo with the Prince and Don Rodrigo.)

MARCELO: Bring forth the tyrannous murderer of my children, that he may die. May his death be the eve of a great and joyous celebration. I will do mercy and justice by marrying off a live daughter and avenging a dead one. Generous Don Sancho, heir of my noble title, come now to meet your future wife if you esteem my house. Leonor, speak to Don Sancho. This is the man I've waited so long to see, that this weary old body might at last find rest.

PRINCE: Give me your hands, my lady.

SANCHO: [*Aside*] Love, you have sentenced me to death!

LEONOR: So you play your tricks in town as well as in the country! I know all about your deceit, your flattery full of lies and mischief.

MARCELO: What are you saying, my clever Leonor? You're either being foolish or you've made a terrible mistake. Speak to Don Sancho.

SANCHO: [*Aside*] He intends to marry Leonor. Heaven give me patience!

LEONOR: Sir, this is Don Sancho; Don Sancho is not the man you thought.

SANCHO: Don Sancho of Portugal humbly kisses your feet.

FABIO: [*Aside*] We've been dealt a trump of Don Sanchos, and what's more, they're all for real! I can't figure out what the prince is after.

PRINCE: Don Sancho of Portugal respects you as his father-in-law.

LEONOR: That man is just a scoundrel who's trying to trick us.

SANCHO: [*To the Prince*] Why do you want to strip me of my glory, my nobility, my very being? If this is a joke, it's gone far enough. If it is love, you must control yourself. You know that I know who you are. If you marry her, you'll marry beneath yourself. She is my equal; let me have her. The stars, sir, have forced me to adore her.

LEONOR: If he is a scoundrel, why is he speaking to him with such reverence?

MARCELO: I am confused. What's happening here?

PRINCE: You cannot possibly love her if you want to deprive her of a kingdom. I love her; be patient.

(Enter Riselo.)

RISELO: Sire, they are coming posthaste to bring you sad news. Your father the king has died, and the whole kingdom awaits you, for

your absence has been discovered. They're coming in search of
you now to take you back.

PRINCE: I shall bring them a queen. Marcelo, embrace me now, unless
you're angry with me for concealing my identity. I am your king.
What are you waiting for? Come here.

SANCHO: And I, sire, must be the first to pledge my obedience to
you. Forgive me, for it was love and jealousy that led my tongue
astray.

MARCELO: My prince and lord, surely you understand that I can hardly
believe my good luck . . .   ·

PRINCE: I mean to be your son-in-law.

MARCELO: What great good fortune! You bring honor upon this house.
This is indeed a happy time. Obedient, submissive daughter, give
his highness your hand.

LEONOR: Since it was heaven's will that you should have one unfortunate daughter, it's only right that the other should be doubly
blessed with luck.

(Leonor gives the Prince her hand.)

MARCELO: I see my blessing manifest in you.

RISELO: Here is Don Diego.

PRINCE: It's only right that he should pay for so many offenses. If
they were less serious, I could pardon them.

*(Enter Don Gil wearing penitential sackcloth with a noose
around his neck, and Don Diego and Domingo.)*

GIL: Prince of Portugal, you who inherit a happy kingdom through the
death of your father, King Alfonso, may he rest in peace; noble
Marcelo; Leonor, whose virtues have made you queen: execute
Don Gil instead; it is not right that Don Diego should die. I have
offended your house and heaven like an irrational beast, for a
sinful man deserves that name. I have been the greatest sinner the
world has ever known, but I trust in God and in my penitence. I
was the devil's slave. I served him in these mountains, committing
unspeakable crimes, raping many virgins. I was proud, but I am
now humble. Because of this change, heaven has shown me its
secrets. Lisarda was disobedient, but she has become so obedient
that she is her father's slave, and God has kept you from knowing
her. She has suffered so much that today she has died of grief,
bemoaning the grave sin for which I alone deserve to be punished.

I was the cause of her harm, not Don Diego, as you thought. As I've told you, she has lived here in these mountains. God has forgiven her; her suffering brought absolution. Henceforth call her Mary the Sinner; let that now be her name. Her body now lies among the myrtles in your garden; her soul has flown up to heaven on wings of penitence. Overcome with shame, I publicly confess my sins, for God has ordered me to accuse myself of them in public. And now St. Dominic's white robe and black cape await me, for I want my penitence to astound the world. I will shout my sins aloud. As a monk in Spain's first religious order, I'll show the world how I've changed.

(Exit Don Gil.)

PRINCE: Don't go, Don Gil! Stop, listen, wait! What a strange turn of events!

LEONOR: I am bewildered.

MARCELO: Is my Lisarda really dead?

(Music plays. A curtain is drawn, revealing Lisarda's corpse kneeling in the garden next to a crucifix and a skull.)[89]

He was telling the truth, holy heavens! She's more beautiful and more perfect than she was in life.

LEONOR: And she's no longer chained or branded.

MARCELO: My curse had its effect, but if God could transform it like this, it's turned out to be a blessing in disguise. Let Don Diego live, and not die.

DOMINGO: Today I've been born again, black beard and all!

DIEGO: These strange events should strike wonder in the hearts of men forever!

MARCELO: Let Lisarda be buried, and let the new queen go to her court, thus concluding this true story.

(They draw the curtain on Lisarda or carry her off on their shoulders.)

THE END.

NOTES TO THE TEXT

1 Cf. Matt. 7:17–20: "... every good tree bringeth forth good fruit. ...; wherefore by their fruits ye shall know them."

2 Cf. I Peter 2:11: "Dearly beloved, I beseech you as strangers and pilgrims, abstain from fleshly lusts, which war against the soul ..."

3 Christ is the Lamb of God. Cf. John 1:29: "The next day John seeth Jesus coming unto him, and saith, Behold the Lamb of God, which taketh away the sin of the world." This is the first of an extraordinary number of animal images in this play (See introduction).

4 The reference is to what the Scholastics called the "sensitive appetite" (a spontaneous, natural inclination towards something), as opposed to the "rational appetite" (=will).

5 According to Scholastic theology, human knowledge is acquired through sense impressions and reason, but angelic knowledge is unmediated and therefore lacks human imperfections such as forgetfulness.

6 In Golden-Age Spain Flora and Lamia were mistakenly thought to have been notorious courtesans of antiquity. Cervantes refers to them as prostitutes in the prologue to the 1605 *Don Quixote*. The pseudo-classical commonplace seems to have originated in Fray Antonio de Guevara's influential *Epístolas familiares* (1539). To the ancients Flora was actually the Italian goddess of flowering plants, and Lamia was a child-stealing nursery bogey. Penelope was Odysseus' faithful wife, who resisted the enticements of many suitors during her husband's long absence at the Trojan war. The Roman matron Lucretia, raped by Sextus Tarquinius, told her husband of her misfortune and then committed suicide rather than live with dishonor.

7 Hero and Leander are the ill-fated lovers of Musaeus' epic of the same name. Leander swam the Hellespont each night to visit Hero, guided by the light in her tower. One night the light was extinguished in a storm, and Leander drowned, whereupon Hero likewise drowned herself. Mira de Amescua wrote a play called *Hero y Leandro* which survives in a manuscript in the Biblioteca Nacional, Madrid. Pyramus loved Thisbe and arranged a rendezvous with her. Finding her bloody scarf at the meeting place, he wrongly assumed she was dead and killed himself. Thisbe likewise committed suicide upon finding Pyramus' body (Ovid, *Metamorphoses* 4, 55–166. The best known treatment of the story in English is the play-within-a-play in Shakespeare's *Midsummer Night's Dream*. Mira de Amescua also used the episode as a play-within-a-play

in the second act of *El ejemplo mayor de la desdicha, y capitán Belisario*.

8 This was probably a popular couplet.

9 Cf. John 1:23: "He said, I am the voice of one crying in the wilderness, Make straight the way of the Lord, as said the prophet Esaias."

10 According to Neoplatonic philosophy, love transforms the lover into the beloved; hence, Lisarda is now transformed into Diego. Here, however, the reference is also to the fact that Lisarda's is going to wear men's clothes in the next scene.

11 Cf. Sebastián de Covarrubias, *Tesoro de la lengua castellana o española*, s. v. "grulla": "At night when they're asleep, and during the day, while they're eating, they post sentinels to warn them if people are coming."

12 According to tradition, Nimrod was the builder of the Tower of Babel, and hence emblematic of pride. Cf. Gen. 10–11.

13 Cf. Ps. 36:7: "How excellent is thy loving kindness, O God! therefore the children of men put their trust under the shadow of thy wings."

14 Cf. Job 14:5: "Seeing his days are determined, the number of his months are with thee, thou hast appointed his bounds that he cannot pass . . ."

15 Cf. Matt. 4:1: "Then was Jesus led up of the spirit into the wilderness to be tempted of the devil."

16 Roland was the hero of the *Chanson de Roland* and of Ariosto's *Orlando Furioso*.

17 These words indicate the approach of dawn. Cf. *Don Quixote* I.20, where Sancho tells Don Quixote: ". . . by the science I learned when I was a shepherd, it can't be more than three hours till dawn, since the muzzle of the Bear is at the top of his head, and at midnight it is in line with the left paw."

18 Icarus was the son of the legendary architect Daedalus. Imprisoned by Minos, Daedalus escaped by making wings of wax for himself and his son, but Icarus flew too near the sun, the wax melted, and he fell into the sea (Ovid, *Metamorphoses* 8.183–235).

19 On the night of Jesus' arrest, Peter denied him three times. Cf. Luke 22:55–57: "And when they had kindled a fire in the midst of the hall, and were set down together, Peter sat down among them. But a certain maid beheld him as he sat by the fire, and earnestly looked upon him, and said, This man was also with him. And he denied him, saying, Woman, I know him not."

20 Cf. Luke 22:60–62: "And Peter said, Man, I know not what thou sayest. And immediately, while he yet spake, the cock crew. And the Lord turned, and looked upon Peter. And Peter remembered the word of the Lord, how he had said unto him, Before the cock crow, thou shalt deny me thrice. And Peter went out, and wept bitterly."

21 Cf. Job, chapters 1 and 2.

22 Cf. Covarrubias, *Tesoro*, s. v. "cigüeña": "The stork symbolizes [filial]

piety, because it takes pity on its parents in their old age, and brings them food to the nest, and takes them out to fly on its wings; I think it was for this reason that the Hebrews gave it the name *chasidah*, which is the same as to say 'pious,' from the noun *chesed*, mercy."

23 The harpies were mythological creatures, part woman, part bird, that snatched away the souls of the dead or seized or defiled the food of their victims.

24 Probably a reference to the popular belief that elephants grew new tusks in old age. See Covarrubias, *Tesoro*, s. v. "elefante."

25 In Golden-Age Spain the Portuguese were stereotyped as outrageous flatterers and greatly susceptible to love.

26 In Greek legend Semiramis was the wife of Ninus, King of Assyria, and founder of Babylon. Her cruelty was proverbial in Spanish Golden-Age literature. Her life is the subject of a famous two-part play by Pedro Calderón de la Barca, *La hija del aire*.

27 Insatiable thirst is a symptom of dropsy (edema).

28 A reference to the Catholic doctrine that Christ is truly present in the communion wafer (Eucharist).

29 Cf. Covarrubias, *Tesoro*, s. v. "elefante": "The elephant is most merciful towards the weak; and thus, when passing through [a flock of] sheep, it gently moves them out of its way with its trunk so as not to trample upon them."

30 The man-hating Amazons were reputed to have slain their fathers, husbands, and male offspring. Aeneas became emblematic of filial piety, because he rescued his father Anchises from the destruction of Troy, carrying him out of the burning city on his shoulders. Cf. *Aeneid* 1, 617; 3, 710ff.

31 Cf. Matt. 5:28: "But I say unto you, That whosoever looketh on a woman to lust after her hath committed adultery with her already in his heart."

32 Milton Buchanan observes in the introduction to his edition of the play (Chicago, 1906) that "the origin of magic in Toledo, and its peculiar relation to a mythical *cueva de Hércules*, are ill-defined; but had not Virgil, Charles the Great, Reineke Fuchs, among others, been sent there by tradition to study the *scientia Toletana*?"

33 The four elements are earth, air, fire, and water.

34 Having sexual relations with two sisters was considered incestuous.

35 The cherubim belonged to the second highest order of angels, ranking just below the seraphim.

36 Perhaps an ironic reference to Jesus' words to Simon (Peter) and Andrew: "Follow me, and I will make you fishers of men" (Matt. 4:19).

37 In the original, S + clavo (nail), i.e., "slave."

38 Cf. Covarrubias, *Tesoro*, s. v. "cocodrilo": "it pretends to sob, thus deceiving passers-by, who think it is a needy and afflicted human person,

and when it sees them approaching it, it attacks and kills them on the
ground." The English expression "crocodile tears" reflects this folk belief.

39 Iphis killed himself when the cruel Anaxarete refused his offer of love.
The gods punished her by turning her into stone. Cf. Ovid, *Metamorphoses* 14:698–771.

40 Beloved of Apollo, the beautiful Daphne rejected him. Her father, the
river god Peneius, turned her into a laurel tree. Cf. Ovid, *Metamorphoses*
1:452–567.

41 The Prince refers to the folk belief that snakes (especially asps) could not
resist the words (or music) of the charmer. Buchanan cites the following
passage from the *Cartas inéditas de Eugenio de Salazar* (1570) in this
regard: "We read of the asp that, so as not to hear the words of the
charmer, it sticks one ear to the ground and covers the other with its
tail."

42 The word "Jew" here is of course not to be taken literally; rather, it is
the ultimate insult. In the racist society of seventeenth-century Spain, the
charge of Jewish ancestry was one of the few weapons peasants could
use against their oppressive masters. It was notorious that in the Middle Ages many nobles had married wealthy converts from Judaism; but
such intermarriage almost never occurred among peasants, so they could
therefore boast of their racial purity.

43 Cacus was the son of Vulcan. He ravaged the countryside with his thiev-
ery, finally even stealing some of the cattle of Geryon from Hercules,
who killed him. Cf. Ovid, *Fasti* 1:543ff.

44 St. Sebastian was a third-century Christian martyr. The Emperor Dio-
cletian ordered him to be stripped, tied up, and shot with arrows. Jet
figurines of religious subjects were common in Golden-Age Spain. Presumably, Domingo compares himself to a jet image because he is so
dirty.

45 The peasant Diego gets the Latin wrong; it should of course be "ora pro
nobis."

46 In the original Spanish, literally, "Galician."

47 Spanish "payo" (=a country bumpkin, a hayseed). Galicia was one of
the poorest and most backward regions in Spain, and its inhabitants were
scorned as ignorant and superstitious.

48 Martha and Mary Magdalen were the two sisters of Lazarus, whom Jesus
raised from the dead. Martha is the prototype of the dutiful housewife,
while Mary Magdalen is famous as a repentant prostitute. Cf. Luke 7:37–
50 and 10:38–41 as well as John 11:1–4. It is generally agreed today that
Mary Magdalen and Lazarus's sister are the same person, although the
Greek Fathers considered them distinct.

49 The gold *escudo*, introduced by Charles V, was the principal monetary
unit of seventeenth-century Spain.

50 Judas betrayed Jesus for thirty pieces of silver. Cf. Matt. 26:15.

51 Herod the Great was the king of Judaea at the time of Jesus' birth; fearing that the newborn child would become King of the Jews in fulfillment of the prophecies, he had all children under two years of age in Bethlehem slain. Cf. Matt. 2:16.

52 Verginius was a plebeian who killed his own daughter to save her from the lust of the decemvir Appius Claudius.

53 This is either a reference to the tyrannical Darius II of Persia (414–405 B.C.), whose misgovernment led to revolts in Syria, Lydia, Media, and Egypt; or to the cowardly Darius III (c.380–330 B.C.), who was stabbed to death by his own followers on Alexander's approach.

54 The Spanish text has "Mandio," but this is surely a mistake; L. Manlius Torquatus, a dictator; or his son, T. Manlius Torquatus, a consul, each of whom, for his severity, was surnamed "Imperiosus."

55 Brutus was a friend and supporter of Julius Caesar, who later betrayed the dictator and became the best known of his murderers.

56 Cf. *Diccionario de Autoridades*, s. v. "pelícano": The pelican "is covered with white and black plumage, except for its breast, on which it has a hard vermilion-colored covering; for this reason it is said that in order to feed its chicks, it wounds its own breast so that they can drink its blood."

57 Atropos="Irresistible," one of the Three Fates or Parcae.

58 The Spanish has "sortijas" but this is probably just for the sake of rhyme with "prolijas." The stage direction in Act II says: "Dale una sortija."

59 See note 43.

60 Cf. Acts 9:15: "But the Lord said unto him, Go thy way: for he is a chosen vessel unto me, to bear my name before the Gentiles, and kings, and the children of Israel . . ."

61 Cf. II Kings 2:11: "And it came to pass, as they still went on, and talked, that, behold, there appeared a chariot of fire, and horses of fire, and parted them both asunder; and Elijah went up by a whirlwind into heaven."

62 Pompey was assassinated in Egypt by order of Ptolemy II; Caesar was assassinated in the Roman Senate; Marius took Rome by storm and embarked on a reign of terror, slaughtering senators and noblemen, but died suddenly of a fever only three weeks after being elected consul for the seventh time; the Emperor Claudius was poisoned by his wife Agrippina; Marcellus, conqueror of Syracuse, was killed in an ambush; Tarquinius, the seventh and last legendary king of Rome, died in exile at Cumae; Mithradates VI, king of Pontus, after murdering his mother, his sons, the sister whom he had married, and his concubines, was overthrown by his own troops. After vainly trying to poison himself, he ordered a Gallic mercenary to kill him; the heroic general Belisarius, envied by the emperor Justinian, was accused of complicity in a conspiracy against the emperor; his fortune was confiscated and he was imprisoned in the

palace.

63 According to Herodotus, Cyrus the Great, founder of the Persian empire, was exposed in the mountains, suckled by a dog, and educated by a shepherd. Artaxerxes, younger son of Xerxes, was raised to the throne of Persia by the vizier Artabanus, the murderer of his father. Viriatus, a Lusitanian shepherd, escaped from the massacre of Galba and rose to become his people's commander-in-chief in their war against Rome. According to Herodotus, Darius the Great won the crown of Persia by a trick of his groom. Sulla rose from poverty to become dictator of Rome. According to Ravisius Textor, Tamerlane rose from being a swineherd in his youth to king of Scythia (*Officina* [Basel, 1616], p. 399). Primislaus, legendary first king of Poland, was of humble origin. The Roman hero Cincinnatus twice left his plow to become dictator of Rome.

64 Solomon began his career as king of Israel by asking God for an understanding heart in order to discern between good and evil and to judge his people rightly (cf. I Kings 3:9). Later, however, he idolatrously worshiped the gods of his pagan wives (I Kings 11:5–8). Origen (c. 185–c. 254), the most distinguished and influential theologian of the ancient church after St. Augustine, castrated himself and was later defrocked for teaching objectionable doctrines.

65 Dimas was the traditional name of the "Good Thief" who repented while being crucified next to Christ (cf. Luke 23:39–43).

66 Paul was at first a fierce persecutor of the Christians but was later converted by a vision of Christ on the road to Damascus (cf. Acts chapters 8–9).

67 According to Ptolemaic cosmology, the earth was surrounded by three concentric spheres or regions: (1) water; (2) air; and (3) fire.

68 Játiva is a town in the province of Valencia.

69 Ribadavia is a town in the west of the province of Orense in Galicia.

70 Laredo and Adra are two famed fishing ports; Laredo is on the Cantabrian coast, and Adra is on the Mediterranean, near Almería.

71 Lycia was a district in the southwest of Asia Minor, occupying the coast between Caria and Pamphylia, and extending inland as far as the ridge of Mt. Taurus.

72 Lycea is the modern Lecce, a town in Apulia, Italy

73 Boeotia was a district of central Greece, bounded by Phocis and Locris on the west and north; by Attica, Megaris, and the Corinthian gulf on the south; and by the Strait of Euboea on the northeast.

74 Arcadia was in Greece, the central district of Peloponnesus, an inland plateau.

75 Transylvania is a high plateau in the extreme eastern portion of Hungary.

76 Dalmatia was a region of the ancient kingdom of Illyria in the northwest of the Balkan peninsula and on the Adriatic Sea.

77 Epirus is an ancient district of northern Greece extending along the Ionian
    Sea from the Acroceraunian promontory on the north to the Ambracian
    gulf on the south, and bordering Illyria, Macedonia, and Thessaly on its
    landward side.
78 Tyre was a famous seaport of Phoenicia.
79 The mythical phoenix was the unique representative of its species.
80 The fourth sphere is the sun.
81 Cf. Revelation 9:12: "And the fourth angel sounded, and the third part
    of the sun was smitten, and the third part of the moon, and the third part
    of the stars; so as the third part of them was darkened, and the day shone
    not for a third part of it, and the night likewise."
82 Cf. Covarrubias, *Tesoro*, s. v. "águila": "the name comes from the Latin
    noun *aquila*, an abbreviation of *ab acumine oculorum*, according to St.
    Isidore. This is because when it is so high in the air that we can hardly
    glimpse it flying over the sea, it can see the fish swimming in the shallow
    water, and it swoops down from on high like an arrow, and carries them
    off in its claws."
83 Cf. Job 14:1–2: "Man born of woman is of few days, and full of trouble.
    He cometh forth like a flower, and is cut down: he fleeth also as a shadow
    and continueth not."
84 Cf. Jer. 18:6: "O house of Israel, cannot I do with you as this potter?
    saith the Lord. Behold, as the clay is in the potter's hand, so are you in
    mine hand, O house of Israel."
85 This whole passage is a gloss on the popular song: "Esclavo soy, pero
    cuyo / eso no lo diré yo, / que cuyo soy me mandó / que no diga que
    soy suyo" ("I'm a slave, but whose slave I'll never say, for my master
    commanded me not to say that I'm his").
86 According to tradition, Christ was given 5,000 lashes in the praetorium.
87 According to Catholic doctrine, a place of natural happiness to which the
    souls of unbaptized infants are consigned.
88 The Spanish contains an untranslatable pun on Domingo's name (=Sun-
    day in Spanish). The servant asks if he must die [on] a wretched Sunday
    (if wretched Domingo too must die), and Riselo answers that he'll not
    die on Sunday but that very day, which is Thursday.
89 This is the iconography with which St. Mary Magdalen was usually por-
    trayed in art.

ACI 4847   3/19/92

THE DEVIL'S SLAVE
(El esclavo del demonio)

Antonio Mira de Amescua

Translated by Michael D. McGaha
Introduction by José M. Ruano

This is a powerful and poetic play in which carnal and spiritual love come under intense examination as a holy man, who preaches piety to others, himself succumbs to lust and makes a pact with the devil. The play bears fascinating parallels with the Faust theme and has important ties with plays by Tirso de Molina and Calderón.

Michael D. McGaha is Professor of Romance Languages and Chair of the Department of Modern Languages and Literatures at Pomona College, Claremont, California. Author of numerous articles on Cervantes and the Spanish theatre of the Golden Age, he has edited *Approaches to the Theater of Calderón* (Lanham: University Press of America, 1982) and is currently editor of the journal *Cervantes*. His critical edition with Introduction and Notes of Lope de Vega's *La fabula de Perseo* appeared in 1985 (Kassel: Reichenberger) and his translation of Lope de Vega's *Lo fingido verdadero / Acting is Believing* (San Antonio: Trinity University Press) was published in 1986.

J.M. Ruano de la Haza is Associate Professor of Spanish at the University of Ottawa. His previous publications include critical editions (with John E. Varey) of Lope de Vega's *Peribáñez y el Comendador de Ocaña* (London: Tamesis Texts, 1980), of Calderon's *Cada uno para sí* (Kassel: Reichenberger, 1982), *El purgatorio de San Patricio* (Liverpool: Liverpool U. P., 1988), and *El alcalde de Zalamea* (Madrid: Espasa-Calpe, 1988). In addition he has had numerous articles on Golden Age drama and the Spanish nineteenth-century novel published in leading journals, has edited *El mundo del teatro español en su Siglo de Oro: ensayos dedicados a John E. Varey* (Ottawa: Dovehouse Editions, 1989) and is the current contributor of the section "Spanish Literature, 1490-1700 (Drama)" of *The Year's Work in Modern Language Studies*. J.M. Ruano is General Editor with Nigel Dennis of *Ottawa Hispanic Studies* (Ottawa: Dovehouse Editions), a series of books on Spanish and Spanish-American language, culture and literature.

Carleton Renaissance Plays in Translation 16 Dovehouse Editions Canada

General Editors: Donald Beecher and Massimo Ciavolella

ISBN 0-919473-46-6